MW00720977

THE
RULES BOOK
2005-2008

THE
RULES BOOK
2005-2008

ERIC TWINAME

REVISED BY BRYAN WILLIS

SHERIDAN HOUSE

Dedication

To my mother and father who taught me the first rule I knew

This edition first published 2005
in the United States by
Sheridan House Inc.
145 Palisade Street
Dobbs Ferry, NY 10522
www.sheridanhouse.com

Printed in Spain by Graphycems

ISBN 1-57409-205-7

CONTENTS

PREFACE

Eric Twiname was an active dinghy sailor, a keen team racer and a Laser National Champion. He liked to look at the rules from the competitor's point of view. He campaigned successfully to get the 720° alternative penalty system into the rulebook (before its introduction, boats had to retire whenever they broke a rule) and he'd have been delighted to see that the two-turns penalty is now the standard penalty system in the main body of the rules. He also tried, unsuccessfully, to get the order of the rules changed to put the sections of most interest to the competitor at the front of the book. Twenty years later the rules were reorganised almost exactly as he proposed.

Eric wrote regular rules articles in the 1970s which were so popular that he used the same comic-strip style for his famous *Rules Book* which he wrote after serving for several years on the Royal Yachting Association's Racing Rules Committee.

It was Eric who persuaded me to join the RYA Racing Rules Committee under the chairmanship of Gerald Sambrooke-Sturgess who, with Greg Bemis from the United States, first developed a set of international racing rules. Eric would be very pleased to see the dramatically simplified rules that came into effect in 1997.

Eric's tragic death in 1980 meant a great loss both to his friends and to racing sailors everywhere. His *Rules Book* has helped countless helmsmen to grasp the principles of the racing rules, and in making the changes necessary for the book to comply with the current rules, I have been careful not to change Eric's unique method of presentation, which is so popular all over the world.

I am grateful to Bengt O Hult from Sweden for checking my updated manuscript.

Bryan Willis

Eric's name and memory live on not only in this book. The Eric Twiname Memorial Trust, a registered charity, helps youngsters start and progress in the sport of sailing. Its address is:

Dinny Reed, Administrator
Eric Twiname Memorial Trust
Sycamore Cottage
Shortheath Common, Kingsley
Borden, Hants GU35 9JS

THE
RULE CHANGES

The major differences between
the 2001-2004 and the 2005-2008
racing rules.

Every year at the Conference of the International Sailing Federation, improvements and amendments are made to the racing rules, but only every four years (in the year following the Olympic Games) are the 'new rules' published. This eighth edition of *The Rules Book* has been revised to include the changes that came into force on 1 January 2005. Most of the changes are for clarification, but some change the way the game is played.

For most sailors, none of the changes are significant and will not affect the way they sail. But to some sailors, and some race committees, some will be important. The best plan is to scan through all the changes and mark those that you think are relevant to you. All changes have been incorporated into the book. If you are new to racing, it is best not to read these changes; who cares how the situation has changed? Get straight into the book!

- The standard penalty for breaking a 'when boats meet' rule (which is the penalty that applies unless the sailing instructions say otherwise) is still the '720'. However it has been renamed and reworded to reflect a change. It is now called the 'two-turns penalty', and provided the two turns are done in the same direction and contain two tacks and two gybes, if it's short of 720 degrees that no longer matters.

- The unnumbered rule 'SPORTSMANSHIP AND THE RULES' is given better prominence to emphasise its importance. A small change of wording has been made to make it clear that when a boat retires after breaking a rule of part 2 (the 'when boats meet' rules), she cannot be disqualified in a hearing for the same breach. (There have been a significant number of protest committees that have disqualified boats in a hearing even though they retired in recognition of breaking a rule in the same incident).

- A boat sailing under the racing rules that meets a boat that is not, must comply with the Collision Regulations. A boat can no longer protest another boat for breaking the Col Regs. Only the race committee or the protest committee can protest.

- Organisers of ocean races often require boats to switch to the Collision Regulations at night. It is now clear that it is the rules of part 2 (when boats meet) which are replaced by the right-of-way rules of the Collision Regulations or by government right-of-way rules.

- When two boats are tacking at the same time, and one is clear astern of the other, neither boat was required to keep clear of the other. Now the boat clear astern must keep clear.

- The 'room at marks and obstructions' rule doesn't apply at a windward mark. That hasn't changed, but there was a problem at a leeward mark when boats were tacking onto a proper course. It could be argued that the rule would not apply there either, which of course is not the intention. New wording (actually the wording from the 1997-2000 rules) is intended to resolve the problem so that sailors can be sure that at every mark other than a windward mark, the 'room at marks and obstructions' rule applies.

- Rule 18.2(c) (regarding the rights and obligations of boats when one is clear ahead of the other as they reach the zone) has been changed slightly to clarify that if the boat that was clear ahead tacks, then the obligation on the boat that was clear astern to keep clear (and give room if she becomes overlapped on the outside) is removed.

- A right-of-way boat that changes course must normally give room to a keep-clear boat to keep clear. When changing course to round or pass a mark, however, she does not have that obligation. This has not changed. What has changed is that she is relieved of this obligation only after the starting signal. This will be important as boats approach and pass the back of the committee boat.

- When beating to windward, a boat needing to tack because of an obstruction (such as the shore) can hail for room to a boat astern or to windward. Nothing new about that. But there was a flaw in the rule that meant if the boat needing room was above close-hauled she didn't have the right to hail; an awkward situation for a boat that had luffed above close-hauled before she realised she needed room to tack. This has been resolved so that the boat may be 'close-hauled or above'. There is a new clause to clarify that to hail for room to tack when in fact there is no safety issue, breaks the rule.

- There is now a requirement for a boat not to interfere with another boat that is on another leg of the course, or, where the course is several laps, on another lap. This is to prevent a boat, that can discard her final race results and needs to prevent her rival finishing in a top position, from skipping a mark. The new wording is not aimed at stopping the tactics of Ben Ainslie in the final Laser race of the 2000 Sydney Olympics (which is still a legitimate tactic), but if the rival slips past, it will stop skipping a mark and manoeuvring against the rival on the next leg. This rule has been in the match and team racing appendices, but now it applies to all disciplines.

- The definitions of a 'party' has been extended to include the 'organising authority', so it is clearer that a boat may seek redress from the protest committee because of an error or omission of the organising authority (in addition to the race committee).

- A national authority (eg the Royal Yachting Association, United States Sailing Association, Australian Yachting Federation), in its 'Prescriptions to the Rules', may now limit the rules permitted to be changed by sailing instructions.

- The definition describing how a boat 'starts' has been revised to clarify that before a boat can start she has to be entirely on the pre-course side of the line, and having complied with the requirements of the 'round-the-ends' rule (if it is in force and the boat was over the line in the final minute).

- There is a requirement for an organising authority to make the Notice of Race (in addition to the sailing instructions available) available to boats.

- The rule that requires a boat to 'sail the course' has been changed so that a boat that crosses the finishing line can nevertheless go back and correct an error in sailing the course, and a boat doesn't finish in a multi-lap course as she sails through the finishing line on each lap, until she has completed the course.

- When the 'black flag rule' is in force for a start, and a boat breaks the rule (by being on the course side during the final minute), and there is a general recall or the race is abandoned, the race committee (at the start line) is now required to display the boat's sail number (in the starting area) before the next warning signal. No signal will be given when a boat or boats are on the course side at the starting signal.

- The provision for an 'S' flag to be displayed on a committee boat before the start to signify that a shortened course is to be sailed, has been removed. The meaning of the 'S flag' displayed from the committee boat at the finishing line is now specified in the rules so that it is unnecessary to specify it in the sailing instructions: between a rounding mark and the committee boat, a line through which boats are required to pass at the end of each lap, or between two gate marks. The race committee may shorten course so that other scheduled races can be sailed.

- The rule describing how a race committee changes a course by signalling at a rounding mark at the beginning of the changed leg, has been revised. The mark at the end of the changed leg need not be in position at the time the change is signalled (this avoids a sailing instruction to this effect). A new signal (green or red triangular flag) is included as an alternative to 'the new compass bearing' being displayed.

- When a mark goes missing or drifts significantly out of position, the race committee may replace it with a mark of similar appearance, or, alternatively, with an object displaying flag M and make repetitive sound signals.

- As from 1 January 2006, trapeze and hiking harnesses must have a device that can quickly release the competitor from the boat at any time while in use.

- The 'outside help' rule has been extensively revised to make clear what outside help is permitted: help when persons or vessel is in danger, help for an ill or injured crew member, help from the crew of the other boat to get clear after a collision; help in the form of information freely available to all boats, and unsolicited information from a disinterested source, which may be another boat in the same race.

- Some of the 'prohibited actions' in rule 42 (Propulsion) have been modified slightly: 'repeated fanning of any sail either by pulling in (was 'trimming') and releasing the sail' and 'repeated rolling of the boat, induced by body movement or by repeated (new adjective) adjustment of the sails or centreboard, or by steering (new)', and sculling has been changed to: 'repeated movement of the helm that is either forceful or that propels the boat forward or prevents her from moving astern (was 'repeated movement of the helm not necessary for steering').

- There are some additions to the 'exceptions' (in other words, these actions are now permitted): 'A boat may be rolled to facilitate steering', 'When a boat is above a close-hauled course and either stationary or moving slowly, she may scull to turn to a close-hauled course' and 'A boat may reduce speed by repeatedly moving her helm'.

- When there is damage or injury that is obvious to the boats involved the requirement for a protest flag for boats over 6 metres is removed. This will avoid protests being found to be invalid for technical reasons when there is damage or injury. It continues to be the case that boats under 6 metres are not required by the rules to display a protest flag.

- There is clarification as to when a protest committee may and may not protest a boat. It can't protest based on information from an interested party, or an invalid protest (unless there has been injury or serious damage). If the protest committee is hearing a valid protest and suspects a third party is to blame, it must adjourn the hearing, inform the third party that the protest committee is protesting her, and then hold the new and adjourned hearings together.

- A protest may be lodged with only a description of the incident provided that the identity of the protestee is established before the hearing.

- It is clearer that a boat may request redress not only if the boat itself is physically damaged but also if a person is injured, when the other boat broke a rule of part 2 ('When boats meet').

- There were always arguments as to which rule applied when there was a conflict between a sailing instruction and a rule in the Notice of Race. There is a new rule that requires the protest committee to '... apply the rule that it believes will provide the fairest result for all boats affected'.

- It is made clear that a protest committee may act on a report from any source when considering opening a 'gross misconduct' hearing. When a competitor has left the venue, the committee must not hold a hearing but may submit a report to the competitor's national authority.

- There has always been a restriction on what bodies can change the rules. National authorities and, more importantly, organising authorities, are no longer permitted to change rule 42 (Propulsion) but there is still no restriction on a class organisation changing rule 42 in their class rules. However, it continues to be the case that national authorities may prescribe that rules may be changed 'to develop or test proposed rules'.

- ISAF (the International Sailing Federation) itself may authorise changes to any racing rule in exceptional circumstances for a specific international event (such as the Americas Cup).

- A national authority may now restrict changes to its prescriptions, so that organising authorities cannot simply write a sailing instruction to say the national prescriptions don't apply.

- The 'notice of race' may be changed if 'adequate notice is given'.

- Gone is the confusing term 'jury' (without the adjective 'international'). Whether appointed by the organising authority or the race committee, the body will be known as a 'protest committee'. (At major international events, the organising authority will still appoint an 'international jury'.)

- Sailing instructions used to have to state which scoring system was to be used for an event. Now if it's not mentioned, it is, by default, the commonly used 'Low Point' scoring system (first gets 1 points, second gets 2 points etc).

- If only the leading boat finishes within the time limit (validating the race for the other boats), but then retires, it was argued that the race should not be scored. It is now clear that it will be.

LEARNING
THE RULES

The rules of sailing are complex. There's no getting away from that. But there are ways of making rule knowledge much more accessible and the rules themselves easier to understand. This book is written very much with those two aims in mind.

A good working knowledge

Anyone who races sailing boats needs to know something about the rules. To begin with you need to know only enough to get your boat around the course without fouling the others. Later, the rules become tactically important because they define what moves you can make when trying to overtake other boats and, just as important, what tricks other people might legitimately use in trying to overtake you.

So the crucial point about learning the sailing rules is that you need a sound working knowledge. There is little point in learning the rules merely to be able to quote chapter and verse. That won't help you on the water, whereas a good working knowledge certainly will, since knowing the rules is a vital part of your racing skills – as important as knowledge of wind and weather.

The International Sailing Federation's (ISAF) racing rulebook is something most people approach at best reluctantly. For one thing it's only usually approached at all when you've got a problem; which puts it immediately into the category of garages, police stations and dentists. But with the difference that, mostly when you turn to the rulebook, you will find something that either you can't quite understand or that contradicts something you thought you knew.

Now that the two-turns penalty is standard, you need to make a decision quickly after an incident: take a penalty or sail on and risk being disqualified after a protest hearing. Making the right decision could determine whether you win a major regatta or championship.

Which rule applies?

This book approaches this problem by looking at real live situations that you're likely to come across while racing. So rather than looking for a rule which might apply to the situation in question, you can turn straight to that situation and read which rule applies, how it applies and why. To make this possible, the situations are arranged here, not in the order set out in the ISAF rule book, but to a logic based on your perception of situations as you meet them on the water.

There are several things that anyone who knows anything at all about sailing will be able to tell you about a collision or near miss, whether they have ever seen a rule book or not. The first thing they'll be able to say is *whereabouts on the course the incident happened.* They shouldn't find it too difficult, either, to say *which tacks the boats were on* (port tack or starboard tack), w*hether they were overlapped, and whether either boat was changing course.* And already, by answering these questions correctly, the majority of racing incidents can be resolved and we are left with, at most, ten per cent. The sections of the book have therefore been arranged to correspond to parts of the course, with subdivisions into incidents where boats are on opposite tacks, on the same tack, changing course or rounding a mark.

In this way, when you are trying to unravel the rights and wrongs of a particular incident, you can quickly home in on the relevant five or ten per cent of possible incidents. Among these, the one you want will be easy to find. Having found it, you can read why one boat is in the right and the other in the wrong, why a particular rule applies, which rule that is and, on difficult points, which appeals cases support the interpretation. The rule referred to can then be looked up in the ISAF Racing Rules of Sailing (reproduced at the back of this book).

Avoiding rule infringements

So far I have only mentioned the book's use in providing a post-mortem analysis after a rule has been broken. But if you're a racing helmsman you constantly need to know just what you can do during a race without breaking any rules. You can certainly build up this knowledge by tearing around the course hitting other boats and being protested against afterwards, but by far the best way to learn is to keep your rule knowledge running in advance of your sailing skills.

Some right-of-way problems are much more common than others, so the racing situations dealt with here have been graded so that you can, if you like, sit down and work up your rule knowledge to a suitable level that fits in with your other racing abilities.

How to use this book

The incidents and situations interpreted in the book are graded on three levels with symbols for quick recognition. These levels are:

1 Rules everyone who races should know (dealt with on pages 11 to 16)

2 Racing at the top end of a club fleet

3 Top-level national and international competition and team racing

For the purpose of learning the rules, the book should not be read from cover to cover in the usual way. That would be too big a bite at once and probably pretty confusing, unless you already know the rules quite well. Instead, the best approach is to decide what level of rule knowledge you want from the book beforehand, then to ignore everything listed beyond the level you've set yourself.

Take the example of a helmsman who has raced for a couple of seasons, and who wants to improve his rule knowledge so that it is at least on a par with the people who are winning his club races. His approach to learning would be to read all items marked by one boat (but not those marked by two boats), checking back to any rules referred to, but ignoring the appeal case references.

If you work this way you needn't read from the front of the book to the back but will learn faster by picking a particular section – mark-rounding from an off-wind leg, for example, – and first studying only that section, rather than trying to take in too much at once. Re-reading, dipping into the book at random – but not yet reading beyond the level you've set yourself – are all useful parts of the learning process. For really keen groups of people, and particularly for young sailors, quizzes are an obvious way of livening up the process.

Learning is also speeded up considerably by using the book as a reference after racing to check the rights and wrongs of any incidents or near misses you experienced during the race. When using the book in this way, of course, you would not restrict yourself to the grading levels, since an incident you want to know about might be one of those rare ones in group 3.

One important word of warning, though. What may look like two identical situations in different sections of the book will sometimes have opposite interpretations. This is because the position on the course is crucial. For example, when two boats collide within two lengths of a mark, the boat in the wrong might be the one that is in the right if you take the mark away and have them in open water on a leg of the course. It is vital to make sure you bear in mind the leg of the course the boats are on – which is why that information is printed at the top of every page.

The interpretations

The interpretations used are, as far as possible, not my own but those of the ISAF. Throughout, I have included references to ISAF's most useful published appeals, so anyone can look these up if they want to. At a protest meeting – whether you are on the committee or one of the warring parties – the relevant appeal case placed on the table is usually decisive. You are instantly a rule expert. No longer is it a question of 'my opinion is this . . .' but 'this is what the definitive ISAF case says', which is difficult for a protest committee to refute, or for a competitor who has just been disqualified to argue about.

The ISAF appeal cases are accepted as definitive throughout the world. Major sailing nations also publish cases resulting from appeals and questions they have decided, to help guide the clubs and race organisers in the area of their jurisdiction. Although national authorities' cases do not have the same 'authoritative' status as the ISAF cases, a protest committee that decides a case contrary to a case published by its own national authority is obviously likely to have the decision overturned on appeal.

Where to obtain the ISAF rules

The rules themselves are revised once every four years and those used in this edition are valid until the end of 2008. These rules together with the RYA prescriptions can be bought in a booklet from the Royal Yachting Association, Romsey Road, Eastleigh, Hampshire SO5 4YA, England. So can the RYA appeals case book. The ISAF racing rules alone and the ISAF Cases can be bought from the International Sailing Federation at Ariadne House, Town Quay, Southampton, SO14 2AQ United Kingdom. The current text of the rules is on the ISAF web site: www.sailing.org.

THE RULES EVERYONE WHO RACES SHOULD KNOW

An understanding of these first few pages of introduction to the rules enables a racing helmsman to keep out of trouble and provides the logical framework which underlies all the 'when boats meet' rules, however complex. These are the most important five pages in the book.

The sailing rules are designed to prevent collisions and to promote fair sailing. So when boats collide, or when a right-of-way boat is forced to steer clear to avoid contact, the boat in the wrong should be penalised. The voluntary penalty is the 'two-turns penalty' (two turns of the boat). If a helmsman in the wrong does not take the voluntary penalty soon after the incident, another competitor or the race organisers may lodge a protest. In the protest meeting the boat in the wrong is disqualified. The basic right-of-way code is quite simple, but it is important to know that the rights and obligations of boats in open water are often different from those at marks of the course or obstructions.

Basic right-of-way in open water
When neither boat is about to pass a mark or an obstruction.

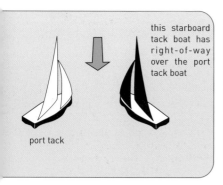

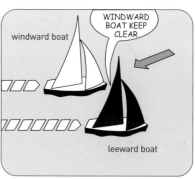

I   A boat on port tack must keep clear of a boat on starboard tack (rule 10).

2   A windward boat must keep clear of a leeward boat (rule 11).

3   A boat which is tacking must keep clear of one that isn't (rule 13).

4   A boat clear astern of another must keep clear of the one ahead when they are both on the same tack (rule 12).

Basic right-of-way at a windward mark

At a windward mark – that is a mark of the course that you have been tacking to get to – the basics are:

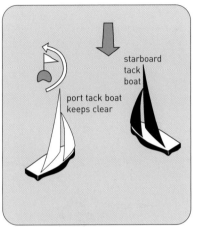

1 When on opposite tacks, take the mark away and apply the principles as in open water (rules 10 and 18.1(b)).

2 When on the same tack, the boat next to the mark must be given room to pass the mark by the boat outside (rule 18.2 (a)).

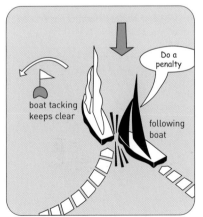

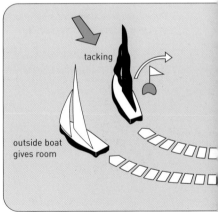

3 When a boat is tacking to pass the mark, she must keep clear of any other boat (rule 13).

4 A boat overlapping on the outside must give room to a boat tacking on the inside (rule 18.2(a) and definition of 'room').

Basic right-of-way at an off-wind mark

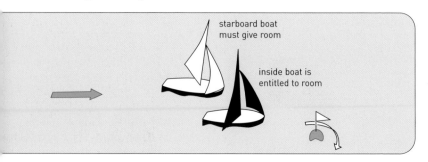

At an off-wind mark – one you have sailed to on a reach or a run – the basics are:

1 If the boat on the inside at the mark is the give-way boat (on port tack if they are on opposite tacks, or to windward if they are on the same tack), she must be given room to pass the mark (rule 18.2(a)).

2 If the boat on the inside at the mark is the right-of-way boat (on starboard tack if they are on opposite tacks, or to leeward if they are on the same tack), the outside boat must keep clear (rule 18.2(a)). But the inside boat must not sail further from the mark than needed to sail her proper course (unless her proper course is not to gybe, and the leeward boat did not establish the overlap from clear astern) (rules 18.2 and 18.4).

3 A boat which approaches the mark clear ahead of another has the right to bear away or gybe round the mark; the other boat must keep clear (rule 18.2(c)).

4 If they are overlapped when one of them reaches the two-length zone, the outside boat's obligation continues even if the overlap is broken later (rule 18.2 (b)).

DEFINITIONS AND TERMS

The rules are built on simple and precise ideas; these are the building blocks and they must be understood if the full meaning of the rules is to become clear.

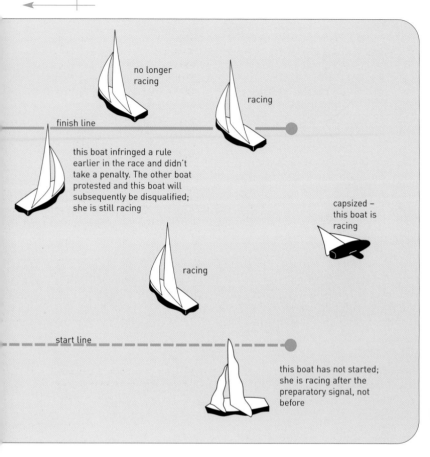

no longer racing

racing

finish line

this boat infringed a rule earlier in the race and didn't take a penalty. The other boat protested and this boat will subsequently be disqualified; she is still racing

capsized – this boat is racing

racing

start line

this boat has not started; she is racing after the preparatory signal, not before

Racing

The racing rules apply to boats that are racing or sailing in or near the racing area and intend to race or have been racing. Penalties for breaking the 'when boats meet' rules come into force at the preparatory signal (usually 4 minutes before the starting signal) and apply to a boat until she has finished and cleared the finish line. A boat not racing (before the preparatory signal or after finishing and clearing the line and marks) is subject to the racing rules but will be penalised only if she interferes with a boat that is racing (Part 2 preamble and rule 22).

A boat which breaks a rule without realising it and which therefore continues racing and is later disqualified after a protest has exactly the same rights under the rules as other boats racing (ISAF Case 1). A boat that continues to race without taking a penalty, knowing that she has broken a rule, violates the basic principle: Sportsmanship and the Rules.

Port tack and starboard tack

A boat is on starboard tack when her starboard side is her windward side. Conversely, a boat is on port tack when her port side is her windward side. However, when sailing directly downwind or by the lee, she is on the tack corresponding to the opposite of her mainsail. Sailors who have problems knowing which tack they are on can usefully paint 'starboard tack' on the starboard side of the boom and 'port tack' on the port side. It saves having to think (Definitions).

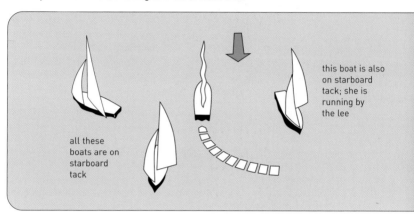

this boat is also on starboard tack; she is running by the lee

all these boats are on starboard tack

Close-hauled

The term 'close-hauled' defines a direction of sailing in relation to the wind; the angle from the wind is different for different classes of boat and to a lesser degree among boats of the same class with different wind speeds, boat speeds, and sailing style.

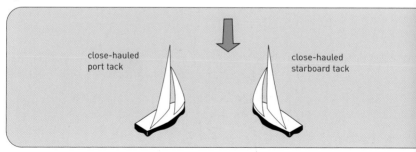

close-hauled port tack

close-hauled starboard tack

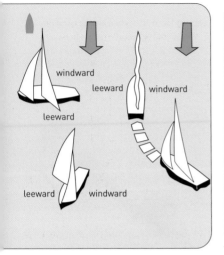
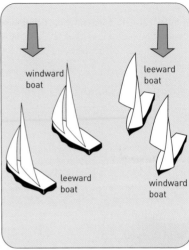

Windward and leeward

'A boat's leeward side is the side that is or, when she is head to wind, was away from the wind. However, when sailing by the lee or directly downwind, her leeward side is the side on which her mainsail lies. The other side is her windward side.

When two boats on the same tack overlap, the one on the leeward side of the other is the leeward boat. The other is the windward boat.' (Definitions)

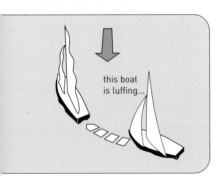
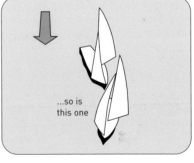

Luffing

A boat is luffing when she is changing course towards the wind. Other phrases commonly used to mean the same as luffing are: 'hardening up', 'pointing up' and 'putting the helm down'.

Bearing away

A boat that is bearing away is changing course away from the wind. Other phrases commonly used are: 'bearing off', 'bearing down', 'freeing off' and 'putting the helm up'.

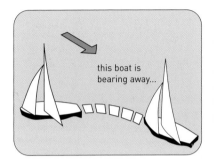

this boat is bearing away...

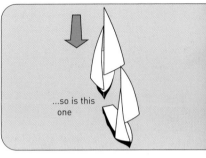

...so is this one

Clear astern and clear ahead; overlap

'One boat is clear astern of another when her hull and equipment in normal position are behind a line abeam from the aftermost point of the other boat's hull and equipment in normal position. The other boat is clear ahead.'

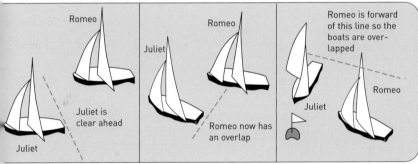

Romeo

Juliet is clear ahead

Juliet

Romeo

Juliet

Romeo now has an overlap

Romeo is forward of this line so the boats are overlapped

Romeo

Juliet

'Boats overlap when neither is clear astern or when a boat between them overlaps both.' (Definitions).

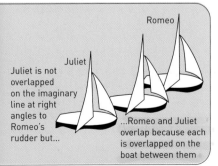

Romeo

Juliet

Juliet is not overlapped on the imaginary line at right angles to Romeo's rudder but...

...Romeo and Juliet overlap because each is overlapped on the boat between them

Romeo

Juliet

Juliet is not overlapped on Romeo here because this time the third boat is not between them

Luffing rights

'Luffing rights' is a colloquial term. A boat is said to have 'luffing rights' over a boat to windward when she has the right to sail above her proper course even if it forces the boat to windward to change course to keep clear. Any leeward boat has luffing rights unless she became overlapped from clear astern within two of her hull lengths. If the leeward boat changes course she must give room to the windward boat to keep clear, and if the windward boat has the right to room at a mark or an obstruction, the leeward boat must give room.

Obstruction

An obstruction is 'an object that a boat could not pass without changing course substantially, if she were sailing directly towards it and one of her hull lengths from it. An object that can be safely passed on only one side and an area designated so by the sailing instructions are also obstructions. However, a boat racing is not an obstruction to other boats unless they are required to keep clear of her or give her room' (Definitions).

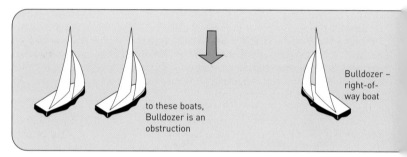

to these boats, Bulldozer is an obstruction

Bulldozer – right-of-way boat

Obstructions include shorelines, heavy patches of weed, fishing nets, shallows (real or perceived), moored boats, tankers, cruising boats and, in some situations, other boats racing.

Mark

A mark is 'an object the sailing instructions require a boat to leave on a specified side, and a race committee vessel surrounded by navigable water from which the starting or finishing line extends. An anchor line and objects attached temporarily or accidentally to a mark are not part of it' (Definitions).

A mark's ground tackle is not counted as part of the mark, but when a boat runs into the mooring line and is drawn on to any part of the mark itself, above or below water, she is counted as having hit the mark.

Starting and finishing

'A boat starts when after her starting signal any part of her hull, crew or equipment first crosses the starting line....' She finishes 'when any part of her hull, or crew or equipment in normal position, crosses the finishing line in the direction of the course from the last mark , either for the first time or after taking a penalty... after correcting an error made at the finishing line.'

Starting is dealt with at the beginning of the section on starting (page 25) and finishing is dealt with at the beginning of the section on finishing (page 80).

Postponement and abandonment
A postponed race is delayed before its scheduled start but may be started or abandoned later.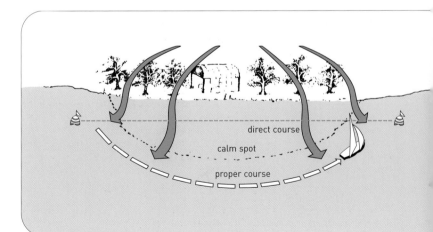

The race committee may abandon a race after it has started only for certain specific reasons. It may reschedule an abandoned race or cancel it. After one boat has sailed the course and finished within the time limit, if any, the race committee shall not abandon the race without considering the consequences for all boats in the race or series (rule 32).

Contact
A collision happens when there is contact between any part of one boat (including all rigging, sails and sheets) or her crew and any part of another boat or her crew.

Proper course
Although a boat is never required to sail her proper course, in some situations a boat is required to sail 'no higher than her proper course' and in certain other situations 'no lower than her proper course'. A proper course is any course a boat would sail to finish as soon as possible in the absence of the other boats referred to in the rule using the term (Definitions).

The reference to 'the other boats referred to in the rule' means that a boat required 'not to sail above her proper course' may, for example, change course to clear her wind or to gain a tactical advantage over a boat or boats ahead or behind.

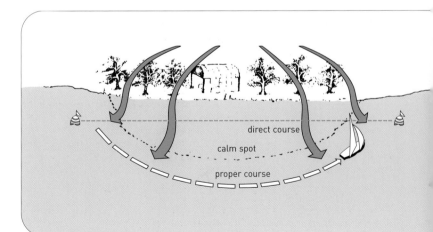

direct course

calm spot

proper course

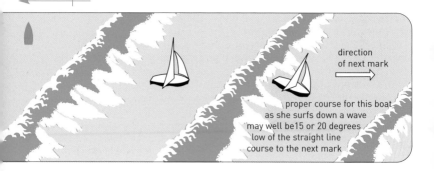

direction
of next mark

proper course for this boat
as she surfs down a wave
may well be15 or 20 degrees
low of the straight line
course to the next mark

Proper course refers to the course the boat makes good and not the direction she is pointing, and provided that it is a reasonable choice, a boat's proper course is whatever her helmsman considers is the best course (ISAF Case 14).

There is no proper course before the starting signal.

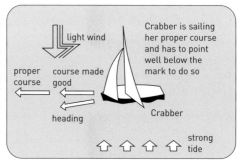

light wind

proper
course

course made
good

heading

Crabber is sailing
her proper course
and has to point
well below the
mark to do so

Crabber

strong
tide

Boat

The racing rules use the word 'boat' to mean any racing sailing boat (sailboards, Optimists, Lasers and 505s, Ocean Racers, Multihulls, remote-controlled models).

THE START

The period covered in this section runs from the preparatory signal until after starting and clearing the starting line.

Starting

A boat *starts* when, having been entirely on the pre-start side of the starting line at or after her starting signal, any part of her hull, crew or equipment crosses the starting line in the direction of the first *mark* (Definition of Start).

Timing of starts

The start of a race is signalled by a 5-minute warning signal, a 4-minute preparatory signal, a 1-minute signal, and the starting signal. The sailing instructions may specify a different time (eg 10 minutes) for the warning signal.

The timing is taken from the visual signals, not from the sound signals, which might fail (rule 26).

From the time of the preparatory signal, until after finishing and clearing the finishing line and marks, breaking a 'when boats meet' rule can be exonerated by doing a two-turn penalty (Definition of Racing and Part 2 preamble).

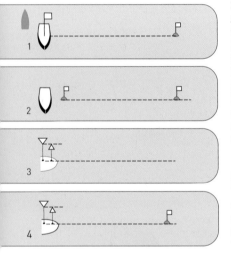

Starting lines

A starting line will usually be one of the following:

(a) A line between a mark and a mast on the committee boat or a place clearly identified in the sailing instructions (1).

(b) A line between two marks (2).

(c) The extension of a line through two stationary posts (3), which may have a mark at or near its outer limit, that boats must pass inside (4).

Inner distance mark (IDM)

On starting lines of types (1), (3) and (4) an inner distance mark may be laid, but this will have an effect only if the sailing instructions state what the obligations of boats are (for example 'boats shall pass between the IDM and the outer starting mark' or 'boats shall not pass between the IDM and the committee boat'). Unless the sailing instructions state otherwise, before you are 'approaching the line from its pre-course side to start', you can pass either side of it (rule 28.2).

Over the line at the start

When any part of a boat, her sails, rigging, equipment or crew is on the course side of the start line at the starting signal, it is said to be 'OCS' (on course side). Usually a boat that is OCS is allowed to return and start properly (rule 29.1).

When one or more boats are OCS, the race committee must make a sound signal and display code flag 'X' unless the only boats on the wrong side are so far over that they will not be confused by the absence of a recall signal.

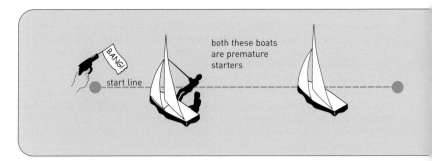

A boat that has crossed the line prematurely must re-start or be scored as 'OCS'. But a premature starter who does not realise her error may be granted redress if she does not return when the visual signal is not accompanied by the prescribed sound signal (rule 29.2 and ISAF Case 31).

When a recalled boat has returned completely to the pre-start side of the start line, she can start correctly. The 'X' flag is lowered once the last of the premature starters has returned to the pre-start side of the line, or four minutes after the starting signal, whichever is the earlier (rule 29.2).

Any boat anchored before the start with part of her ground tackle on the course side of the start line at the start signal becomes a premature starter because the anchor and warp are part of the boat's equipment (rule 29.1).

When code flag 'I' has been displayed as the preparatory signal, any boat whose hull, equipment or crew is on the course side of the start line during the minute before the start must sail back around either end of the line before starting (she can't just dip back over the line) (rule 30.1).

When code flag 'Z' has been displayed as the preparatory signal, any boat whose hull, equipment or crew is in the triangle formed by the starting line and the first mark during the minute before the start will be penalised with a 20% penalty unless the race is postponed or abandoned before the starting signal. If there is no 'general recall' she will be scored as 'OCS' unless she returns and starts properly (rule 30.2).

When the 'black flag' has been displayed, any boat whose hull, equipment or crew is in the triangle formed by the starting line and the first mark during the minute before the start will be disqualified without a hearing, and if the race is restarted, she cannot start in the restarted race (rule 30.3).

Hitting a starting mark

A boat which makes contact with a starting mark after the preparatory signal must immediately sail clear of other boats and sail one turn, including a tack and a gybe. If she believes she was forced to hit the mark because of another boat breaking a rule, she need not do the turn. If a boat hits a mark and in the same incident breaks a 'when boats meet' rule, she may exonerate herself by immediately sailing clear and taking only a two-turns penalty.

The two-turns penalty for breaking a rule before the start signal

When a boat breaks a 'when boats meet' rule after the preparatory signal, she may exonerate herself by taking a 'two-turns penalty' at the first reasonable opportunity after the infringement. This means sailing clear of other boats to find a space, and while keeping clear, turning the boat twice in the same direction including two tacks and two gybes. (The two-turns penalty is dealt with in detail on pages 86–7.)

Breaking a rule just before the starting signal will therefore result in a much more severe penalty than an infringement soon after the preparatory signal. If a boat breaks a rule just before the starting signal and is also OCS, she must get clear and do her turns as soon as possible, then return behind the line and re-start.

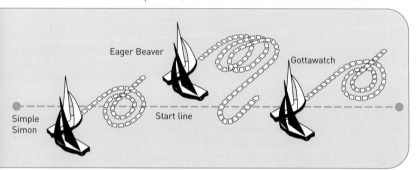

It is two seconds after the starting signal and all these port-tackers have broken rule 10. They must do their turns as soon as they can. Eager Beaver was OCS at the start and will have to go back behind the line and start after completing her turns; Gottawatch started before she broke a rule so she can take her turns and sail on; Simple Simon starts as he commences his turns so he too can complete his turns and sail on.

Anchored, moored, tied up or still ashore

A boat may be disqualified for being ashore, moored or tied up after the preparatory (4-minute) signal (rule 45). If she doesn't sail about in the vicinity of the starting line at some time between the preparatory and starting signals or does not start, she is scored 'DNS' (did not start) (Appendix A).

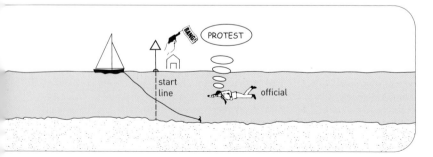

A boat may be anchored after the preparatory signal or held by a member of the crew standing in the water, and no rule is broken (rule 45). However, if an anchor is on the course side of the line at the starting signal, the boat will be scored OCS.

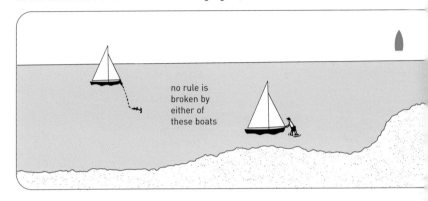

no rule is broken by either of these boats

General recall

When the race officer can't identify boats that are OCS, or when the start is un-satisfactory in some other way, he can make a 'general recall' signal by flying the First Substitute and making two more sound signals after the starting signal.

The procedure when the race officer is ready to re-start is:

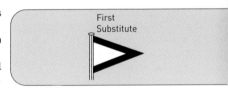

First Substitute

1 First Substitute is lowered with a sound signal.
2 After one minute, a new warning signal is made (with a flag and sound signal).

Any boat which breaks a rule in the race in which the start is abandoned is not barred from competing in any subsequent starts unless the boat was on the course side of the starting line in the minute before a 'black flag' start (rules 30.3 and 36).

Postponement

A race may be postponed by flying the Answering Pennant. The warning signal is made one minute after the Answering Pennant is lowered, accompanied by a sound signal. If there is to be a long delay, the race committee can add a numeral pennant under the AP to indicate the number of hours delay, counted from the scheduled starting time.

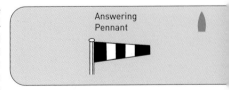

Answering Pennant

RIGHT OF WAY

No room at a starting mark

When approaching the line to start, a windward boat (White) is not entitled to room from any leeward boat (Black) at a starting mark that is surrounded by navigable water (rule 18.1(a)).

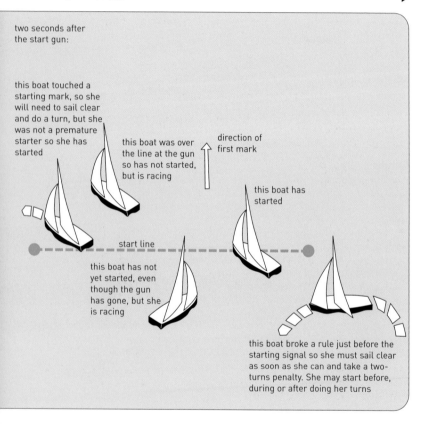

two seconds after the start gun:

this boat touched a starting mark, so she will need to sail clear and do a turn, but she was not a premature starter so she has started

this boat was over the line at the gun so has not started, but is racing

direction of first mark

this boat has started

start line

this boat has not yet started, even though the gun has gone, but she is racing

this boat broke a rule just before the starting signal so she must sail clear as soon as she can and take a two-turns penalty. She may start before, during or after doing her turns

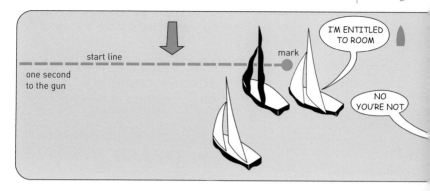

White is not entitled to room but if Black luffs, she must give White room to keep clear (rule 16). With the mark so close, if Black luffs now, White would not be able to keep clear without hitting the mark, so Black must not luff.

If the leeward boat is sailing above close-hauled at the starting signal and she became overlapped from clear astern, she must immediately bear off to close-hauled (assuming that the first leg is a beat) (rule 17.1 and the definition of Proper Course).

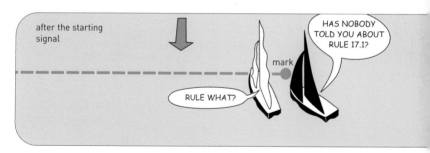

In the to-ing and fro-ing in the minutes before the start, a windward boat is entitled to room at a starting mark; the 'no room' rule applies only when approaching a start-ing mark to start (if the starting mark is surrounded by navigable water) (rule 18.1).

At the port end of the starting line, if the mark is surrounded by navigable water, the leeward boat is not entitled to 'room' but as she is the right-of-way boat, she may sail as high as she likes provided that if she luffs she gives the windward boat room to keep clear (rules 11 and 16).

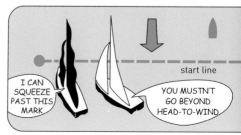

The position is quite different if the starting mark is not surrounded by navigable water or the line's length is limited by, say, a pier. A windward boat is then entitled to room at that mark or pier (rules 18.1 and 18.2(a)).

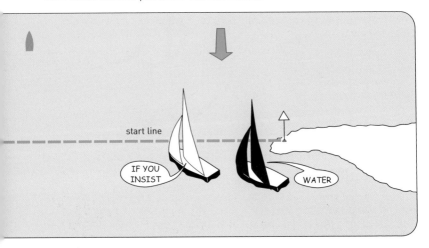

Changing course to start

A right-of-way boat that changes course must give a keep-clear boat room to keep clear. Here Go-getter luffs up to close-hauled to get a good start, but hits a port-tacker that was keeping clear. Go-getter must take a penalty (rule 16.1).

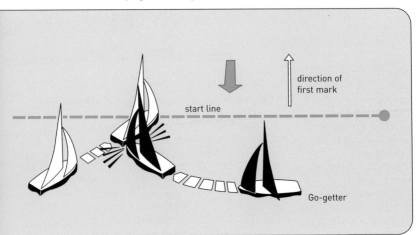

Luffing before the start

Before the starting signal, any leeward boat may luff up to head-to-wind. (If she passes beyond head-to-wind, she'll be changing tack). However, any change of course must be such that the windward boat is able to keep clear. If there's something to windward of the windward boat preventing her from responding, the leeward boat might not be able to luff at all (rule 16.1).

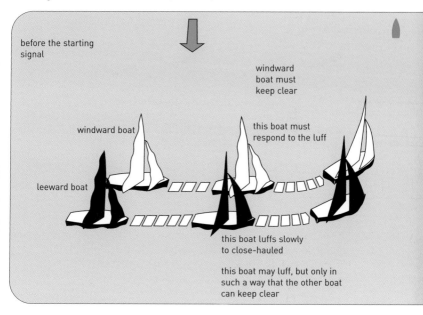

before the starting signal

windward boat must keep clear

windward boat

this boat must respond to the luff

leeward boat

this boat luffs slowly to close-hauled

this boat may luff, but only in such a way that the other boat can keep clear

If for example, the windward boat was 'hove-to' (not moving and sails not drawing) when the luff began, she must be given time and space to pull her sail in, gather way and respond to the luff. The leeward boat has to give her this opportunity. It is important to remember that the first movement of the windward boat's stern in responding to a luff is inevitably towards the leeward boat. The windward boat would not be disqualified in a pre-start luffing incident if she made every reasonable effort to avoid the leeward boat's luff from the moment the luff began.

When more than one boat is overlapped and the leeward boat luffs, they must all respond, each responding to the luff of the boat immediately to leeward, but each leeward boat must luff in such a way that the boat to windward is able to keep clear.

Over the line at the start

While a boat that has been scored OCS (on the course side at the start) is sailing the course, she carries her normal rights. But at the moment she begins heading back towards the starting line, she must keep clear of boats that are not returning. The normal right-of-way rules apply between two boats both returning (rule 20.1).

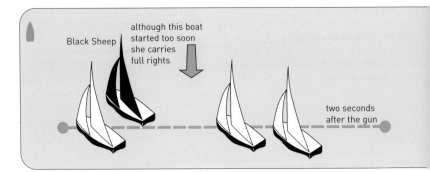

Black Sheep lets her sails flap to slow down, but she maintains her rights until she is heading back towards the line or its extension (rule 20.1).

Once back on the pre-start side of the line, Black Sheep gets back her rights, but she must give any keep-clear boat a chance to keep clear (rules 15 and 16).

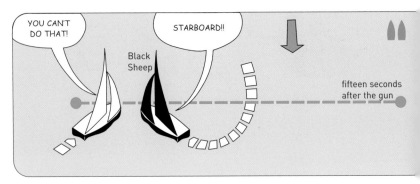

Black Sheep has changed course too quickly and not given the port tack boat room to keep clear. On this showing, Black Sheep's return to the fold would result in her having to do a two-turns penalty.

When the race committee displays code flag 'I' as the preparatory signal, any boat whose hull, equipment or crew is on the course side of the start line or its extensions during the minute before the start must sail outside one end of the line and then start. She may not just dip back over the start line (rule 30.1).

Starting from the wrong side of the line

Cowboy enjoys right-of-way for two seconds more, then loses it as soon as the gun goes if she is caught with any part of the boat or crew on the wrong side of the line at the gun (rule 20.1). If she gets behind the line a second after the gun, she must not be in a position where the white boats cannot keep clear without having to anticipate Cowboy suddenly becoming the right-of-way boat (rule 15).

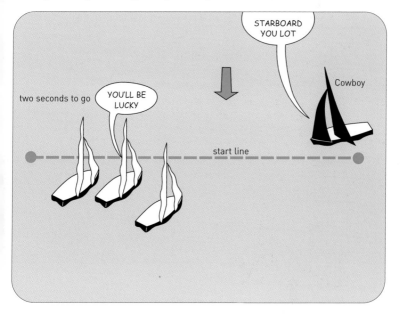

Overtaking to leeward

This is very common before and at the start, though the rules that apply are much the same as those that apply at any other time in the race.

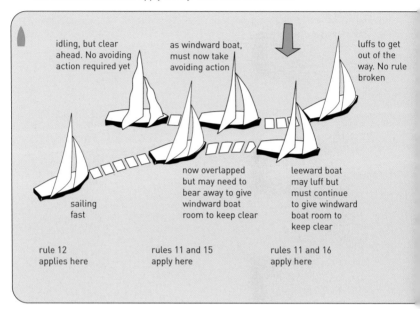

idling, but clear ahead. No avoiding action required yet

as windward boat, must now take avoiding action

luffs to get out of the way. No rule broken

sailing fast

now overlapped but may need to bear away to give windward boat room to keep clear

leeward boat may luff but must continue to give windward boat room to keep clear

rule 12 applies here

rules 11 and 15 apply here

rules 11 and 16 apply here

Moving backwards

A boat moving backwards (through the water) by backing a sail must keep clear of one that is not (rule 20.3).

WINDWARD LEG

A windward leg is one that a boat can complete only by putting in at least one tack.

OPPOSITE TACKS

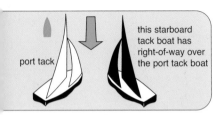

this starboard tack boat has right-of-way over the port tack boat

port tack

Port and starboard

A port tack boat must keep clear of a starboard tack boat (rule 10).

When a close-hauled starboard tack boat bears away to miss the port boat's stern and protests, and there is no collision, the port tack boat's helmsman must satisfy the protest committee that his boat would have kept clear had the starboard tack boat held her course (ISAF Case 50).

The right-of-way boat is required to avoid contact, but if there is no damage, the right-of-way boat cannot be penalised if she gave room to the port tack boat to keep clear. If there is damage which the right-of-way boat could have avoided (provided it is not serious) the right-of-way boat may do a two-turn penalty to exonerate herself (rules 14 and 44.1).

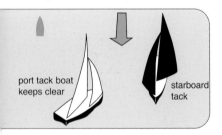

port tack boat keeps clear

starboard tack

The keep-clear boat is, obviously, also required to try to avoid contact. If there is contact, provided there is no serious damage, the keep-clear boat may absolve herself by taking just one turns penalty to cover the whole incident (rule 44.4(b)). If either boat causes serious damage that she reasonably could have avoided, she must retire.

If the helmsman of a starboard tack boat doesn't want the port tack boat to tack on her lee bow, he may hail 'hold your course' and sail under her stern but the hail itself does not place any obligation on the port-tacker. The port tack boat may keep clear however she likes.

A starboard tack boat sailing free has right-of-way over a close-hauled port tack boat. But if the starboard tack boat changes course, she must give room to the port tack boat to keep clear (rules 10 and 16.1).

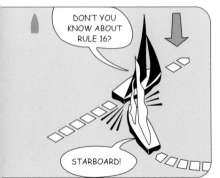

DON'T YOU KNOW ABOUT RULE 16?

STARBOARD!

Port and starboard when the starboard tack boat changes course

A port and starboard incident where the starboard tack boat changes course towards the port-tacker is quite different from the straightforward port and starboard case above. This situation is controlled by rule 16, which says that any right-of-way boat changing course must give the other boat room to keep clear.

The white boat on starboard is in the wrong because she changed course when the port boat was properly keeping clear, and gave no chance to the port-tacker to react to the new situation. Rule 16 doesn't stop the boat on starboard changing course when approaching a boat on port, provided there is room for the port tack boat to keep clear (rule 16.1), and provided that the port tack boat isn't forced to immediately change course in response to the starboard tack boat's change of course (rule 16.2).

Rule 16.1 can have the effect of preventing the starboard tack boat from taking advantage of a windshift. To use the windshift as a defence in a protest hearing, Black would have to satisfy the protest committee that the starboard tack boat's change of course gave her no opportunity to keep clear (rule 16.1).

Port and starboard when the starboard tack boat has just tacked

'When a boat acquires right of way, she must initially give the other boat room to keep clear...' (rule 15)

If there was a protest, Jack-in-the-box would have to satisfy the protest committee that the tack was completed far enough from the other boat for her to be able to keep clear without having to anticipate the completion of Jack-in-the-box's tack.

Calling 'starboard'

There is no obligation to call 'starboard' when you are on starboard tack and a port tack boat is approaching, but it's often a good idea if you think he hasn't seen you. If there is an incident he might have to take a penalty, but you might lose a lot of time by getting tangled up with him.

The starboard tack boat on the right breaks no rule by hailing 'starboard', and then tacking.

A boat that hails 'starboard' when on port tack with the intention of intimidating an inexperienced skipper whose boat is on starboard tack would break the 'fair sailing' rule (rule 2 and ISAF Case 47).

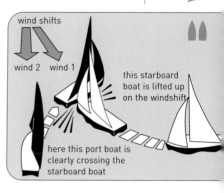

this starboard boat is lifted up on the windshift

here this port boat is clearly crossing the starboard boat

wind shifts

wind 2   wind 1

DO YOUR TURNS

STARBOARD!

Jack-in-the-box

Jack-in-the-box's tack is made too close for the other boat to respond. Jack-in-the-box is in the wrong

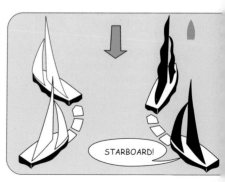

STARBOARD!

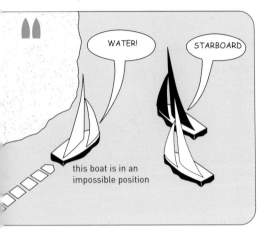

Opposite tack boat requiring room for an obstruction

There is, curiously, no way that a port tack boat which is prevented from tacking by an obstruction can legitimately force starboard tack boats to tack and give her room. Only when she is on the same tack can she hail for room. Here, the port and starboard rule (10) applies, in spite of the fact that the port tack boat's only escape may be to bear away hard or go aground.

SAME TACK

Windward and leeward

When two boats on the same tack are close-hauled and overlapped, the windward boat must keep clear, even if the one to windward cannot sail as close to the wind as the leeward one (rule 11).

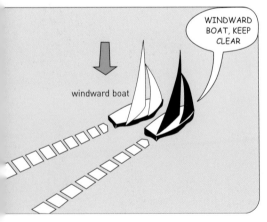

The leeward boat may not sail above her proper course (close-hauled here) unless she has luffing rights. She has luffing rights if she got into this over-lapped position by any way other than from clear astern (rules 11 and 17.1). If she luffs, she must give the windward boat room to keep clear (rule 16.1).

The crew or helmsman of the leeward boat may not deliberately reach out, sit out or trapeze with the intention of hitting the windward boat. This would be penalised under the fair sailing rule (rule 2 and ISAF Case 73).

Luffing

The black boat got her overlap by tacking into this position so she has the right to luff, right up to head-to-wind.

However, while she was tacking she was the keep-clear boat, and she has tacked into a right-of-way position, so she has to initially give the other boat room to keep clear (rule 15).

Then she may luff. If she does, she must give the white boat room to keep clear (rule 16.1).

The white boat must keep clear (rule 11).

Both boats must try to avoid contact (rule 14).

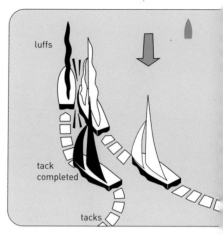

Bearing away

Provided the leeward boat isn't made to change course to avoid hitting the windward boat, the windward boat may bear away below close-hauled as White does here. But as windward boat she must keep clear (rule 11).

The windward boat would not be allowed to do this on an off-wind leg because rule 17.2 forbids it.

If the leeward boat has luffing rights (the right to sail above her proper course), she can luff at any time, but if she does, she must give the windward boat room to keep clear (rule I6.1).

Calling for room at a continuing obstruction

If Mud Tickler carries on she'll hit the shore; if she tacks she'll hit the white boat. The rules provide a way out of this dilemma provided both boats are on the same tack and Mud Tickler is close-hauled (or above): Mud Tickler can hail 'room to tack', or something similar at the white boat.

The white boat must respond immediately either by:

1 tacking as soon as possible or

2 hailing 'you tack' (rule 19.1).

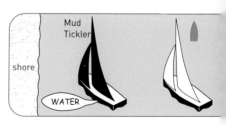

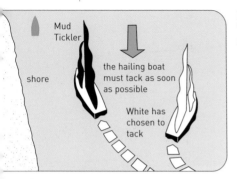

If the white boat chooses to tack, Mud Tickler must tack as soon as possible (rule 19.1(a)).

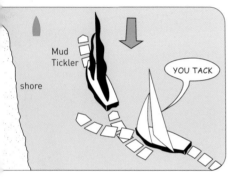

White may prefer to let Mud Tickler tack, keep out of her way and really squeeze into the shore herself. Then White must call 'you tack' and avoid Mud Tickler.

As soon as White has made her 'you tack' call, Mud Tickler must tack as soon as possible (rule 19.1 (b)).

Problems can arise when 'short tacking' against a tidal stream. Whether the inside boat has the right to hail for room hinges on how far apart the boats are when she needs to tack. There is no set number of boat lengths – the distance will vary according to the conditions and the type of boat – but the criteria for deciding are quite clear. The inshore boat is not entitled to hail for water when:

1 she can tack out from the shore and back again on to her original tack without any risk of forcing the outside boat to change course or

2 she can tack and bear off behind the other boat without difficulty.

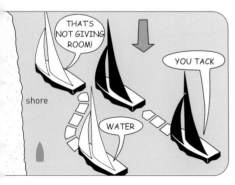

If White is able to tack out from the shore and back on to her original tack without Black being forced to alter course to keep clear, then White has no right to hail for room. Black must still respond to the hail (for example by hailing 'you tack') and may then protest. However, if the protest committee is satisfied that it was reasonable for White to believe she could not tack with the possibility of not being able to keep clear of Black, then White's hail will be ruled as valid. Here White was forced to fall back on to starboard tack before getting to close-hauled on port tack. Black did not give room and must do a two-turns penalty (rule 19.1).

In this sequence (right), White's call was dubious, but as she believed she was going to find it difficult to tack and clear Black, she had the right to hail for room to tack.

Black took a chance by hailing 'you tack' but, as it turned out, White was able to tack and bear off behind Black without difficulty, so there was no rule broken (rule 19.1).

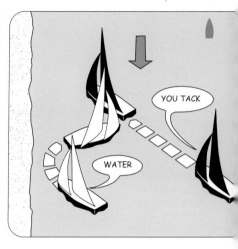

Calling for room at a non-continuing obstruction that is not a mark

A non-continuing obstruction is one that can be passed on either side and requires a boat not less than a length away to make a substantial change of course to miss it. Moored boats, minuscule islands, capsized boats, a right-of-way boat, may all be non-continuing obstructions (the definition is on page 22).

Once the 'room to tack' call has been made here by Black, White must respond exactly as in the section above (rule 19.1). The fact that White would have missed the obstruction anyway doesn't matter, she must respond. Nor does it matter that Black chose to tack rather than bear off and go to leeward of the obstruction. There is no rule that dictates that a boat should take the shortest route around an obstruction. Although if Black needed to make only a small change of course when one length away, the rules don't allow her to call for water to tack: she must then make the course change, staying on the same tack (definition of Obstruction).

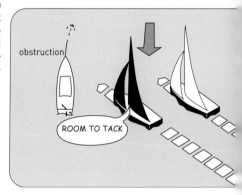

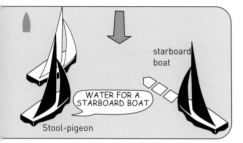

A starboard tack boat as an obstruction

One of the most common obstructions to a close-hauled boat on port tack is a boat on starboard tack.

Stool-pigeon is entitled to hail for room to tack, and the white boat must either tack immediately or call 'you tack' and give room. Stool-pigeon has to see this situation coming in good time or she'll be too late to call and won't be able to get out of the starboard-tacker's way (rule 19.1 and definition of Obstruction).

When Stool-pigeon calls clearly for room to tack, in good time, and White fails to respond, the responsibility is entirely White's and no blame falls on Stool-pigeon for White's failure to tack. However, if there is no response to the first hail, Stool-pigeon must hail again more loudly (ISAF Cases 3 and 54).

Instead of tacking, Stool-pigeon can choose to bear away astern of the starboard boat, since an obstruction can be taken on either side, but she must then give enough room to White if she needs to take action to avoid the starboard boat and wishes to go underneath (rule 18.2(a) and definition of Obstruction).

If White asks for water to bear off behind the starboard boat at the same moment as Stool-pigeon asks for room to tack, Stool-pigeon's call governs. White gets room only if Stool-pigeon chooses not to hail for room to tack, in which case Stool-pigeon must give room whether or not White asks for it (rules 18.2(a) and 19.1).

Forcing another boat to overstand a weather mark

The team racing ploy of holding an opponent on the same tack to sail beyond the lay line and overstand the weather mark is explained on page 66.

TACKING

Tacking ahead of another boat

A boat which is tacking is required to keep clear of other boats until she is on a close-hauled course (rule 13).

Even when the tacking boat has completed her tack she is not necessarily in the clear. She mustn't tack into a right-of-way position (for example, clear ahead) if the other boat cannot keep clear without having to anticipate that she'll be there. So if

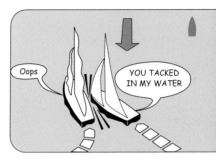

the other boat cannot keep clear without having to begin to change course starting from the moment the tacking boat is on a close-hauled course, the tacking boat has broken the rule (rule 15). In the situation (above) the tacking boat has clearly broken a rule (13 or 15).

In the situation below, White becomes the right-of-way boat when she is on a close-hauled course. Black was able to keep clear without having to anticipate, and she kept clear, so no rule was broken.

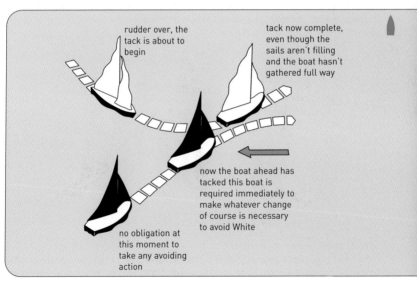

Tacking in the water of a port tack boat

It is not possible to tack as close to another boat when going from starboard tack to port as it is when going from port to starboard.

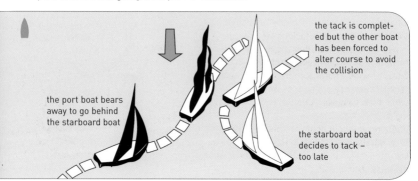

the port boat bears away to go behind the starboard boat

the tack is completed but the other boat has been forced to alter course to avoid the collision

the starboard boat decides to tack – too late

While White is luffing up to head-to-wind, she is on starboard tack. As she is changing course she is required to give room to Black to keep clear (rule 16.1). In this picture Black can easily keep clear by luffing. If White passes through head-to-wind, she becomes the keep-clear boat and remains the keep-clear boat until she is close-hauled on the new tack (rule 13).

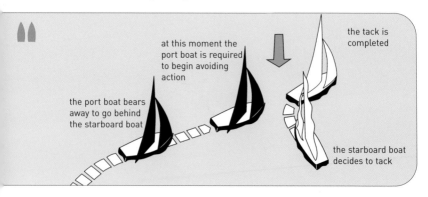

at this moment the port boat is required to begin avoiding action

the port boat bears away to go behind the starboard boat

the tack is completed

the starboard boat decides to tack

White could cross ahead of Black and Black must keep clear. But White might have a tactical reason for wanting to be on port tack, and want to encourage Black to tack.

At the moment White's tack is completed, Black must take whatever avoiding action is necessary to avoid White. By tacking ahead or to windward of Black, Black will be encouraged to tack as Black will not want to sail close astern of White, or in her wind shadow. However, if Black is forced to avoid White by starting to keep clear before White has completed her tack, White will have broken rule 13. In practice, if Black thinks White has not broken rule 13, she will luff and tack before White's tack is complete so as not to spend any time in White's bad air.

When the port-tack boat is steering a course astern of the starboard-tack boat, if the starboard-tack boat (white) changes course, the port-tack boat (black) must be able to keep clear without having to alter course immediately to keep clear (rule 16.2).

Simultaneous tacking

When two boats are tacking at the same time, the one on the other's port side keeps clear (rule 13). However, until they pass head-to-wind, they are on their original tacks. Once they are both through head-to-wind, then whoever is on the right is in the right.

As long as both boats are between head-to-wind and close-hauled, then the one on the other's port side must keep clear. In dinghies and small keel-boats it can be risky to tack immediately after crossing close ahead of a port tack boat – especially if the port tack boat has borne away to miss the starboard-tacker's stern, since she'll be moving extra fast during a tack.

MARK ROUNDING

The mark-rounding rules come into effect when boats are 'about to pass the mark', and continue until the mark is left astern.

Where the mark-rounding rules come into force

There are special rules that apply to passing or rounding marks and obstructions (rule 18). This section is about passing or rounding marks; passing obstructions is dealt with in the sections on windward legs and off-wind legs.

The mark-rounding rules come into force when the leading boat of a pair (or bunch) is 'about to pass' the mark. This is usually at about two or three boat-lengths but in heavy seas or with a tidal stream increasing the boat's speed over the ground, or when the boats are fast catamarans, or when a big bunch of boats is coming together at the mark, this distance could be much more. The mark-rounding rules apply until the mark has been 'passed', that is, left astern on the new leg with no danger of hitting it (rule 18.1).

There is an important 'two-length zone', which is the area around a mark (or obstruction) within a distance of two hull lengths of the boat nearer to it. This is often referred to as 'the circle', but in fact it's an arc for the approaching boats, not those who are saying goodbye to the mark.

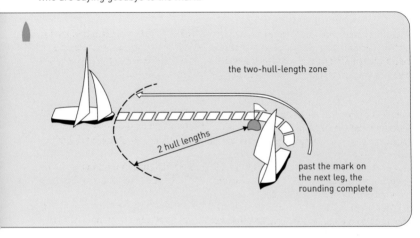

the two-hull-length zone

2 hull lengths

past the mark on the next leg, the rounding complete

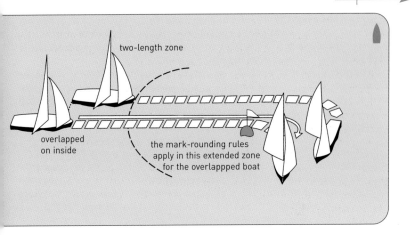

The most usual case where the area in which the mark-rounding rules apply extends further back than two lengths is when several boats are overlapped and the outside boats are required to give room as the boats are 'about to pass the mark' which may mean having to start giving room well before the two-length zone.

The penalty for touching a mark

A boat is counted as touching a mark when any part of her hull, crew or equipment touches it. So a neat hand-off or a spinnaker sheet touching a flag on the mark is a touch. The mark's mooring line or chain is not counted as part of the mark (definition of Mark).

A boat is exonerated for hitting a mark if she sails well clear of all other boats as soon as possible and remains clear while making a turn, including a tack and a gybe (or a gybe and a tack) (rule 31.2).

When a boat hits the 'wrong' side of a mark (sails the wrong side of it and hits it) she must go off and do her turn, and then come back and round it on the right side. If, however, there are no other boats about, she can do her turn round the mark without getting in anyone's way, and fulfil both requirements in one move.

If a boat has gained a significant advantage in the race or series by touching a mark, she must retire (rule 44.1).

Forced on to a mark by another boat

When a boat is forced on to a mark by another boat that has broken a rule, the mark-hitter need not take a penalty. If there is a protest (eg by the mark-hitter or the wrong-doer) and the wrong-doer is penalised (whether or not it was the boat that was protested), then the mark-hitter will be exonerated.

If a boat hits a mark, and breaks a 'when boats meet' rule, (for example because she takes room to which she is not entitled) she can be exonerated from both infringements by doing just one two-turns penalty. However, if she gained a significant advantage, she must retire (rule 44.1).

In the rare event of a mark being submerged by a boat sailing over it, then shooting out of the water to hit a following boat, this boat need not take a penalty. She can't protest against the mark, but she can protest against the boat that caused its irregular behaviour. However, she is still obliged to go to the correct side of it, no matter where it surfaces.

Rights and obligations of a boat which has just hit a mark

A boat that misjudges her mark-rounding and makes contact with the mark must begin to get well clear of other boats as soon as possible, and then promptly make one turn including one tack and one gybe. She retains all her normal rights until she is well clear of other boats. If she is taking the penalty at the finishing line and she is on the post-finish side of the line after doing the turn, she must return completely to the course side of the line before finishing.

If she has gained a significant advantage in the race or series by touching the mark, the option of taking a penalty is not open to her and she must retire, even if taking the penalty would set her back more than she'd gained (rule 31.2).

Rounding a mark in the wrong direction

After rounding a mark the wrong way, the mistake can be corrected by unwinding. To do this correctly, a string representing the boat's wake must, when drawn tight, lie on the required side of the mark (rule 28.1). You don't lose any rights, just because you're going back to unwind or are in the process of unwinding.

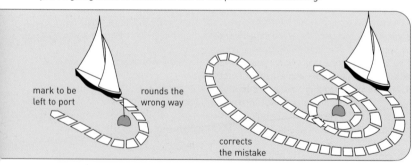

mark to be left to port   rounds the wrong way   corrects the mistake

A mark is only a mark of the course for the leg

A mark is only a mark of the course for a particular boat when it begins or ends the leg of the course on which that boat is sailing (rule 28.2). So on the leg from mark 3 to mark 4, mark I can be hit without penalty, and between a boat rounding mark I on her way to mark 2, and a boat coming down from mark 3 to mark 4, rule 18 (Rounding and Passing Marks and Obstructions) does not apply; the boat rounding has no special rights.

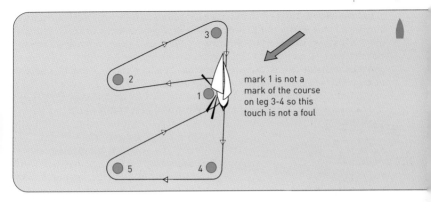

mark 1 is not a mark of the course on leg 3-4 so this touch is not a foul

Mark missing or moved

The race committee should return a drifting mark to its stated position if possible. If that isn't possible they must replace it by a new one with 'similar characteristics' or a buoy or boat displaying Code flag 'M' and make repetitive sound signals (rule 34).

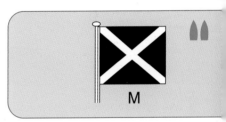

ROUNDING AT THE END OF AN OFF-WIND LEG

Room at a mark

A windward boat which is overlapped with others outside her has the right to room at the mark, provided the overlap is established before the leading boat enters the two-length zone (two of the leading boat's lengths from the mark) and provided that, when the inside boat establishes the overlap, the outside boat is able to give room (rule 18.2(a)). The explanation of an overlap is on page 19.

If the leading boat is unable to give room when the overlap is first established, the inside boat is not entitled to it (rule 18.2(e)). In other words she can't expect an outside boat to do the impossible. This can happen where a group of boats are in line abreast and can-

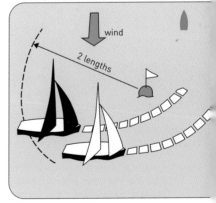

not shift aside fast enough to accommodate a late inside overlapper. When boats are planing in at high speed, it is often impossible for an outside boat to give room when the overlap is established close to the two-length zone.

If there is doubt as to whether the inside boat that was clear astern established the overlap in time (either in time for the outside boat to be able to give room, or before the outside boat reached the two-length zone) then they must assume the boat claiming room is not entitled to it. Circumstances where a helmsman is unable to give room because he isn't properly in control of his boat are not included: a helmsman's incompetence or inexperience is no defence.

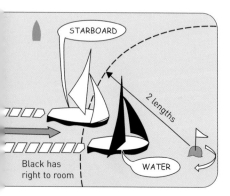

Port and starboard at an off-wind mark

Once the boats are 'about to pass' the mark, the 'rounding and passing marks' rules apply (rule 18).

Here the black boat on port tack is on the inside. She had an inside overlap when the leading boat reached the two-length zone. White must give her 'room to round or pass the mark'. 'Room' is the 'space a boat needs in the existing conditions while manoeuvring promptly in a seamanlike way' so White must give Black room to gybe (rule 18.2 and definition of Room).

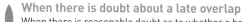

When there is doubt about a late overlap

When there is reasonable doubt as to whether a boat, which comes from clear astern claiming to have established the inside overlap, has established it in time, then the boats must presume she has not (rule 18.2(e)).

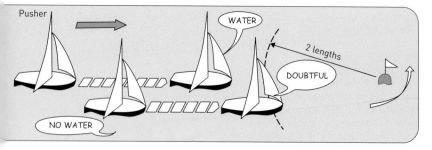

Pusher would find it very difficult to establish that her inside overlap was made soon enough. A witness in another boat or ashore might clinch it, but even so, Pusher would be foolish in this situation to round on the inside and risk being protested. Because of the 'when there is reasonable doubt' rule, Pusher doesn't have the right to room. If the outside boat readily concedes that Pusher has established the overlap in time, then that's a different matter; Pusher would be entitled to pass inside (rule 18.2(e)).

When there is doubt that an overlap has been broken

Here, two overlapped boats are approaching a mark and just before entering the two-length zone, the outside boat claims that the overlap has been broken. But if there is 'reasonable doubt', then the boats must presume the overlap still exists and the inside boat has the right to room (rule 18.2(e)).

If the inside boat disputes a marginal 'clear ahead' claim, the outside boat would be stupid to try and push her luck by denying room to the inside boat.

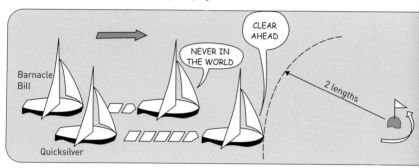

Quicksilver would be hard pushed to win a protest if she didn't give room at the mark, but if she can stay ahead of Barnacle Bill, until the mark is astern of BB, then she will have fulfilled her obligations to give room (rules 18.2(e) and 18.2(b)(c)).

Hailing for room

The rules don't require a hail, but a hail that there is or isn't an overlap, made well before the two-length zone, often avoids disagreement and panic when it comes to who should be doing what at the mark.

How overlaps operate when boats are making a wide rounding

In a big fleet it often happens at a leeward mark that boats round very wide at the end of a downwind leg so that they come in close to the mark. If a boat goes so wide that she enters the two-length zone at right angles to the oncoming fleet, the whole fleet is entitled to room – they are forward of the line at right angles to her aftermost point. They won't all be able to make use of their right to room, but some might be able to, as Interloper might be able to do here.

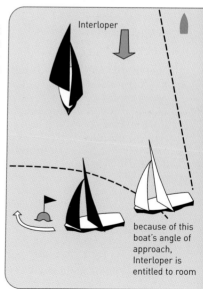

because of this boat's angle of approach, Interloper is entitled to room

Losing the right to room when a boat is carried past a mark by a current or tidal stream

A boat that enters the two-length zone and leaves it has to re-establish her rights when she re-enters the two-length zone.

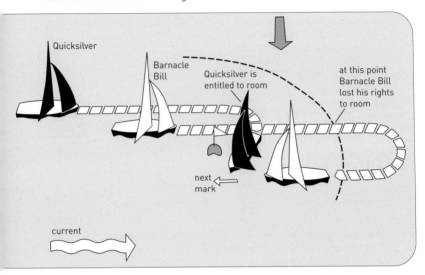

The same principle applies in really windy conditions when a skipper chooses to tack round instead of gybing and during his tack sails past the mark and outside the two-length zone. He must establish new rights on re-entering the two-length zone.

How much room must the outside boat give?

If the outside boat is the keep-clear boat (because she is on the same tack as the inside boat and is to windward, or on opposite tacks and she is on port tack) then she must keep clear, and the inside boat may sail the course she would have sailed in the absence of the outside boat (her 'proper course'). Furthermore, if the boats are on the same tack, and the inside boat is to leeward, and the inside boat established the overlap in any other way than from clear astern, and her proper course at the mark does not include a gybe, then she may luff at any time during the rounding of the mark, right up to head-to-wind, provided she luffs in such a way that she gives room to the windward boat to keep clear.

If the outside boat is the right-of-way boat, then the amount of room she must give is 'the space the inside boat needs in the existing conditions while manoeuvring promptly in a seamanlike way' (definition of Room). This often means the inside boat cannot sail the course she would have sailed in the absence of the other boat. She might like to sail in wide and come up tight on the mark, but if that is taking more room than that required to round in a seamanlike manner, then she hasn't the right to take that amount of room if there is a right-of-way boat on the outside.

More room is needed in rough weather. Although an inexperienced helmsman cannot count on any extra space to allow for his lack of skill, any doubt in a protest will usually go in favour of the inside boat.

White's rounding here, in which she sails wide for purely tactical reasons, breaks rule 11 (windward boat to keep clear). The dividing line between what is a 'seamanlike' rounding and a rounding made primarily for maximum tactical gain can be a fine one. If there's a protest, the outside boat will need to satisfy the protest committee that she gave sufficient room, and the inside boat failed to keep clear. In this situation Black would win the protest. One and a half lengths given by Black was plenty of room and White failed to keep clear.

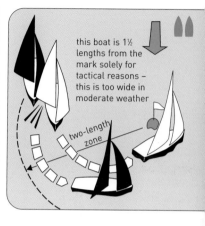

this boat is 1½ lengths from the mark solely for tactical reasons – this is too wide in moderate weather

two-length zone

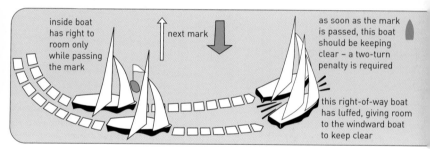

inside boat has right to room only while passing the mark

next mark

as soon as the mark is passed, this boat should be keeping clear – a two-turn penalty is required

this right-of-way boat has luffed, giving room to the windward boat to keep clear

The mark is passed when it is left astern with no chance of colliding with it. When the mark is passed, the inside boat's right to room expires (ISAF Case 25).

Breaking an overlap inside the two-length zone

An outside boat which is required to give room because of an overlap established before entering the two-length zone must keep clear if she becomes clear ahead inside the two-length zone (rule 18.2(b)).

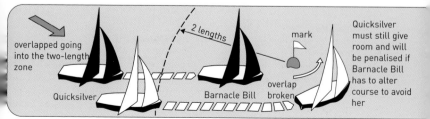

overlapped going into the two-length zone

2 lengths

mark

Quicksilver

Barnacle Bill

overlap broken

Quicksilver must still give room and will be penalised if Barnacle Bill has to alter course to avoid her

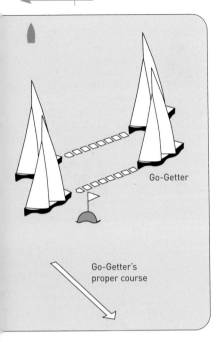

When the inside boat needs to gybe round a mark

When the inside boat's proper course includes a gybe then until she gybes she must take no more room than that required to sail a proper course, even though she is the right-of-way boat (rule 18.4).

The windward boat must keep clear (rule 11).

Even if Go-Getter has luffing rights (because the windward boat established the overlap to windward of her), once they're 'about to pass', Go-Getter must not sail further from the mark than necessary to sail her proper course (rule 18.4). The windward boat must keep clear (rule 11).

When the inside boat has luffing rights and there is a proper course she can sail without gybing

When the inside boat, of two overlapping boats, did not get her overlap from clear astern (so she has luffing rights), and there is a proper course she can sail without gybing, then she may sail straight past the mark, or luff at any time if she gives room to the windward boat to keep clear.

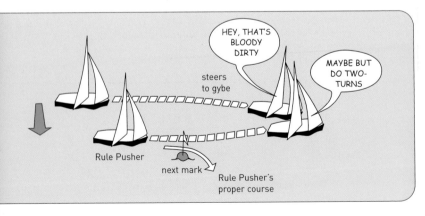

Forcing another boat to the wrong side of a mark

Luffing another boat the wrong side of a mark is rarely wise in normal fleet racing but is often a good tactic in team racing when, by taking one of the opposite team to the wrong side of a mark, a team-mate is able to slip by.

For a leeward boat to be allowed to luff a windward boat to the wrong side of the mark, the leeward boat must have luffing rights, and neither boat must be 'about to pass' the mark. It is difficult to say exactly at what distance from a mark a leading boat is 'about to pass'. It would be at least two lengths even with flat water, not much wind, no spinnakers to douse and no favourable tidal stream. If there was a protest and the protest committee thought it was reasonable for what would have been the inside boat to assume they were about to pass the mark, then it would give that boat the benefit of the doubt.

If, during the luffing process, either boat comes within the 'about to pass' distance, then the leeward boat must immediately bear off to round the mark and if the windward boat is inside, give room.

No hail is required, though it is often worthwhile in order to avoid contact (rules 16.1, 11, 17.1 and 14).

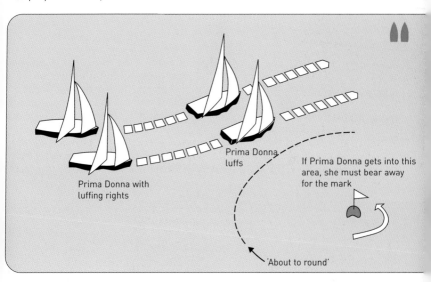

Prima Donna luffs

If Prima Donna gets into this area, she must bear away for the mark

Prima Donna with luffing rights

'About to round'

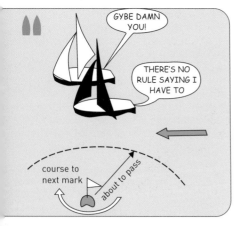

Using starboard rights to sail a boat the wrong side of a mark

When two boats are on opposite tacks the starboard boat may sail any course and the port boat must keep clear (rule 10 and ISAF Case 9). This means that provided both boats remain outside the distance they would be 'about to pass' the mark, the starboard tack boat may take the port boat the wrong side of the mark. No hail is necessary but if the starboard tack boat changes course, she must give the port tack boat room to keep clear (rules 10 and 16).

Passing a mark in opposite directions

When boats are passing a mark in opposite directions the normal 'when boats meet' rules apply, even though the right-of-way boat might be passing on the wrong side. When a boat is 'unwinding' because she passed the mark the wrong way, she maintains her rights.

In these circumstances the boats are not 'about to pass on the same side', so rule 18 does not apply.

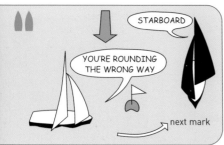

ROUNDING AT THE END OF A WINDWARD LEG

On opposite tacks – port and starboard

When boats on opposite tacks are about to pass a windward mark, the rules apply essentially as though the mark wasn't there (rules 18.1(b) and 10).

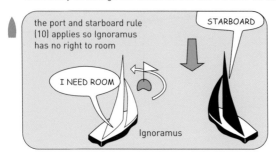

A starboard tack boat can sail in a straight line beyond the mark perfectly legitimately to put a port tack boat about (ISAF Case 9).

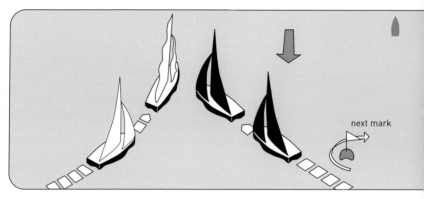

The rule that says a right-of-way boat changing course must give the keep-clear boat room to keep clear, applies in a port-and-starboard situation at the mark (rule 16).

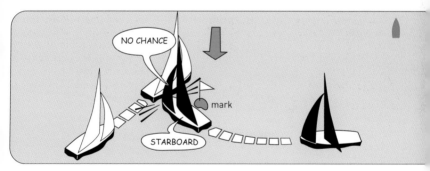

On the same tack - room at the mark
When two boats are overlapped on the same tack, the mark-rounding rules apply in the same way as for an off-wind mark.

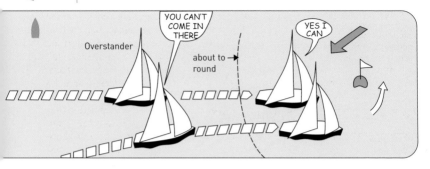

Outside the two-length zone, Overstander is required to keep clear as windward boat (rule 11). But as soon as the leading boat is 'about to round or pass the mark', the rules that apply to marks come into play. If Overstander has an overlap when the leading boat reaches the two-length zone, then the leeward boat must give Overstander room – that is 'the space a boat needs in the existing conditions while manoeuvring promptly in a seamanlike way' (rule 18.2(a) and the definition of Room).

This does not give the right to Overstander to sail an 'enter wide to round up tight to the mark' course. While they are overlapped, she remains the keep-clear boat and is entitled to room only for a 'seaman-like rounding', not a 'tactical' rounding.

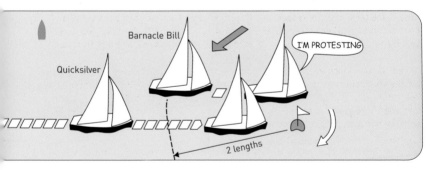

Barnacle Bill is clear ahead on entering the two-length zone so at the mark Quicksilver must keep clear and is not entitled to room. In the two-length zone it is irrelevant that Barnacle Bill becomes the windward boat here because the rule about passing marks (rule 18) takes precedence over the windward/leeward rule (rule 11).

A leeward boat with an inside overlap on entering the two-length zone and below the lay line is entitled to luff round the mark because, even if she doesn't have the right to sail above her proper course (because she established the overlap from clear astern) to luff above close-hauled may be her proper course (rule 18.2(a)).

When both boats approach a mark on the same track with one clear ahead of the other on entering the two-length zone, the boat ahead may luff to head-to-wind but must keep clear from the moment she passes head-to-wind to the moment she is close-hauled on the new tack. If she tacks on to port tack, and the other boat is still on starboard tack, she'll have to continue to keep clear (rules 13 and 10). The boat clear astern may luff to prevent the boat ahead from tacking, provided she is given room to keep clear (rule 16.1)

A leading boat which enters the two-length zone clear ahead may slow down, forcing the boat astern on to the outside. The boat now on the outside must continue to keep clear (rule I8.2(c)). Foiler does nothing wrong here. She is entitled to slow down, and when Thruster gets an outside overlap she must continue to keep clear of Foiler and give her room, including room to tack.

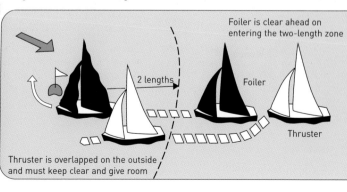

Tacking within the two-length zone

Risktaker completes her tack inside the two-length zone. While she was on port tack she had to keep clear of Speedy approaching on starboard tack. When Risktaker passed head-to-wind, she changed tack, and she was probably clear ahead, but rule 13 says she must keep clear until she is close-hauled. Now, to add to her worries, if Speedy gets an overlap to leeward at any time during the rounding, Risktaker must give room (and Speedy can sail her proper course around the mark). And Risktaker must not force Speedy above close-hauled to avoid contact (rule 18.3). Furthermore, Risktaker has no protection from rule 15 which normally requires a boat that establishes right-of-way (for example by getting an overlap to leeward) to initially give the other boat room to clear.

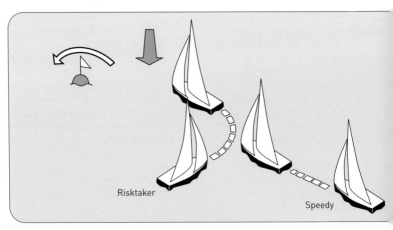

Risktaker

Speedy

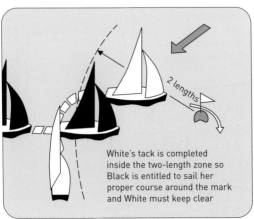

2 lengths

White's tack is completed inside the two-length zone so Black is entitled to sail her proper course around the mark and White must keep clear

A special case of room to tack when the windward mark is big

This covers the unusual case where the windward mark is also an obstruction.

If White cannot lay the mark (pass it without tacking) then she must respond to the hail by either:

1 tacking immediately
2 hailing 'you tack' and give room for the black boat to tack.

If she tacks, no rules have been broken and there are no grounds for protest.

If White thinks she can lay the mark without tacking (she may luff and squeeze round, provided she doesn't pass head-to-wind), she need not respond to Black's hail, but if she fails to lay the mark she must do a two-turns penalty (rule 19.2).

Black should hail early enough to leave room to escape in case White chooses to try to lay the mark; if Black hits the mark and White succeeds in laying it, Black must do a single turn penalty; if Black hits the mark and White fails to lay it, Black may sail on, and may protest White if she doesn't retire or take a penalty.

A special case on a port hand rounding

Both Complacent and Ricochet must keep clear of Starboard under rule 10 while on port tack and under rule 13 while tacking. Ricochet should have acted sooner by hailing Complacent for room to tack to keep clear of Starboard (or bearing away to pass astern of Starboard, in which case Ricochet, as the outside boat under rule 18.2(a), was required to give Complacent, the inside overlapping boat, room to do the same). In the situation shown, Ricochet has left it too late to do that. If, in responding to Ricochet's hail, Complacent collides with the mark, Ricochet will be in the wrong for forcing another boat to break a rule. If Ricochet doesn't do a two-turns penalty, Complacent may protest.

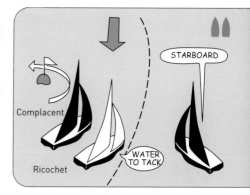

Sailing another boat past a mark
This is a manoeuvre used in team racing and, accidentally, by beginners in fleet racing.

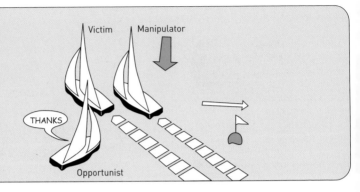

If they are team racing*, there is no rule to stop Manipulator sailing as far beyond the weather mark as she likes, forcing Victim to overstand and letting Opportunist round ahead (ISAF Case 15). Manipulator and Opportunist would be team mates and Victim would be pushed behind Opportunist. Victim is, however, the right-of-way boat. Manipulator must keep clear, even if Victim luffs. If Victim luffs she must give room to Manipulator to keep clear (rules 11 and 16).

[*In fleet racing, Manipulator's actions would have to be consistent with achieving her best finishing position in the race or series (rule 2).]

OFF-WIND
LEG

When boats are running
or reaching.

OPPOSITE TACKS

Port and starboard

A boat on port tack must keep clear of a boat on starboard tack (rule 10). This is a basic right-of-way rule.

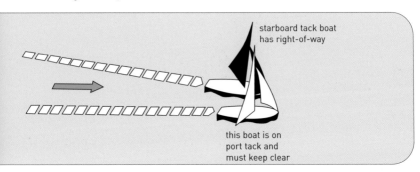

starboard tack boat has right-of-way

this boat is on port tack and must keep clear

The starboard tack boat may sail towards the port tack boat (her 'proper course' is irrelevant) but if she changes course she must give the port tack boat room to keep clear (rule 16.1).

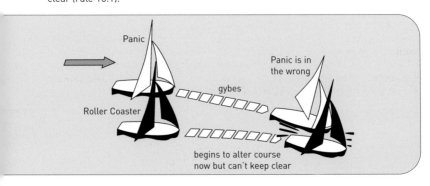

Panic

Panic is in the wrong

gybes

Roller Coaster

begins to alter course now but can't keep clear

When a keep-clear boat does something to become a right-of-way boat, she must initially give the other boat room to keep clear. In the first position, Panic is the keep-clear windward boat, required to keep clear (rule 11). She mustn't sail below her proper course unless she gybes (rule 17.2). She decides to gybe, and becomes the right-of-way boat on starboard tack. Roller Coaster must keep clear (rule 10) but Panic must initially give room to her to keep clear (rule 15). If Panic doesn't do a two-turns penalty, a protest by Roller Coaster is likely to succeed. Had Panic been on starboard tack all along, and made the change of course shown in the diagram, Roller Coaster would be in the wrong (rule 10). The starboard tack boat is allowed to sail any course she likes provided that if she changes course, she gives 'room to keep clear' to the port tack boat (rules 10 and 16.1).

Not overlapped

In open water the port and starboard rule (10) applies even when boats are not over-lapped. The rule which says that a boat clear astern keeps clear of a boat ahead (rule 12) applies only when both boats are on the same tack.

White thinks that because Black is clear astern, Black should keep clear, but in this case the white boat is wrong and must do a two-turns penalty (rule 10). However, if there is damage, the black boat also will have to do a penalty (rule 10). She should have avoided contact (rule 14).

Room to pass a continuing obstruction

The normal basic rules apply between two boats passing a continuing obstruction such as a shoreline (if on the same tack, clear-astern keeps clear of clear-ahead, windward keeps clear of leeward). However, a keep-clear boat is entitled to room on the inside if at the time she gets the overlap there is room for her to pass between the right-of-way boat and the obstruction (rule 18.5).

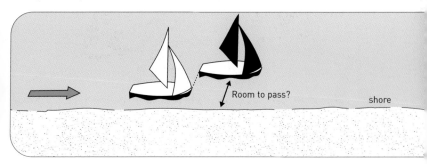

Room at an obstruction which is not continuing

The same as for 'Off-wind Same Tack' (page 70).

SAME TACK

 Windward boat keeps clear
A windward boat is required to keep clear of a leeward boat (rule 11).

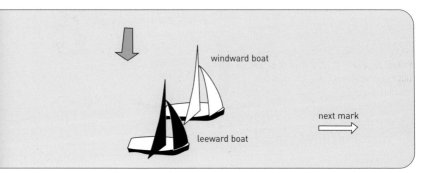

When a leeward boat is sailing her proper course (explained on page 21) and is forced to change course to avoid a windward boat, the windward boat is in the wrong. The rule is an important one, but in some situations it may be overridden depending on how the overlap was established. These overriding situations are dealt with in this section.

Sailing below a proper course
A boat within two of her hull lengths of another must not sail below her proper course when the other boat is on the same tack and is steering a course to leeward of the boat ahead, or is overlapping to leeward (unless she gybes) (rule 17.2).

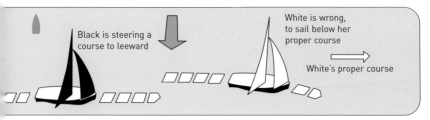

A protest by Black here would be successful if she could establish that White was sailing below her (White's) proper course. It is normal, though certainly not essential, for the leeward boat to give the boat bearing down a warning shout and only protest if the boat ahead, or to windward, continues to sail below her proper course. Black's protest would be dismissed if White can satisfy the protest committee that her course could reasonably be argued as being a 'proper course', which in practice is usually the case.

Overtaking another boat

Because they are on the same tack, the boat clear astern is required to keep clear (rule 12).

More often the overtaking boat doesn't follow exactly in the wake of the boat ahead, but becomes overlapped to leeward.

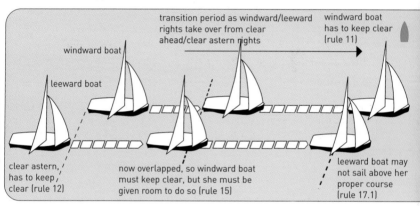

windward boat has to keep clear (rule 11)

transition period as windward/leeward rights take over from clear ahead/clear astern rights

windward boat

leeward boat

clear astern, has to keep clear (rule 12)

now overlapped, so windward boat must keep clear, but she must be given room to do so (rule 15)

leeward boat may not sail above her proper course (rule 17.1)

The obligation on the boat astern to keep clear switches off as the overlap is established. The windward/leeward rule then takes over and the windward boat is required to begin any necessary avoiding action, but the leeward boat must initially give her room to keep clear and in addition must not sail above her proper course. The windward boat may well have to sail above her own proper course to fulfil her obligation to keep clear (rules 12, 11, 15, 17 and ISAF Case 14).

Overtaking more than one boat

A boat clear astern is entitled to sail into an overlapped position between two boats ahead only when there is enough room for her to pass between them at the time the second overlap is established (rule 18.5, ISAF Cases 16 and 29).

The gap is not big enough for Chancer to sail right through so she will have no right to room if she pushes her nose in (rule 18.5).

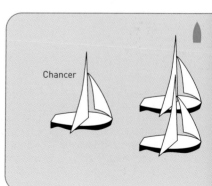

Chancer

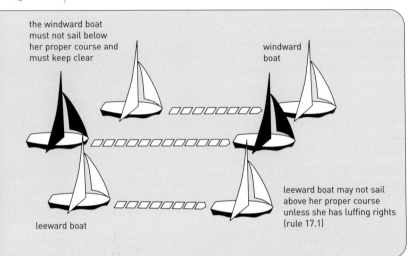

the windward boat must not sail below her proper course and must keep clear

windward boat

leeward boat

leeward boat may not sail above her proper course unless she has luffing rights (rule 17.1)

Black is entitled to sail into the gap because she is overlapped with the leeward boat (which counts as a continuing obstruction) and at the precise moment that she gets an overlap with the windward boat, there is enough room for her to sail right through (rule 18.5, definition of Obstruction, and ISAF Case 29).

This time the windward boat is slightly back from the leeward boat, though still overlapped. Prudence therefore first overlaps the windward boat, without overlapping the leeward boat.

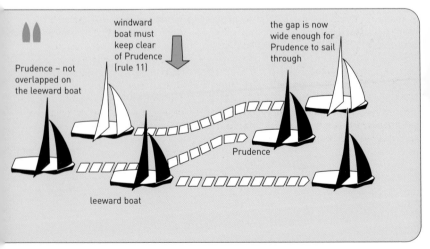

windward boat must keep clear of Prudence (rule 11)

the gap is now wide enough for Prudence to sail through

Prudence – not overlapped on the leeward boat

Prudence

leeward boat

Assuming that Prudence established her overlap to leeward of the windward boat from clear astern, she must sail no higher than her proper course. But her proper course is to sail to windward of the boat ahead so the windward boat must widen the gap to give her room. It would be just the same as if the leeward boat was something sticking out of a shore line; they are both continuing obstructions (rule 18.5).

Room to pass a continuing obstruction

A boat clear astern is entitled to room to sail into a gap between a boat ahead and a continuing obstruction, such as a shoreline, only when, at the moment the overlap is first established, there is enough room for her to sail through the gap (rule 18.5).

this boat is entitled to room between the other boat and the shore because there was room for her to sail through the gap when she first established the overlap (rule 18.5)

shoreline

this boat is the right-of-way boat but must give room because the inside boat gained a legitimate overlap (rule 18.5)

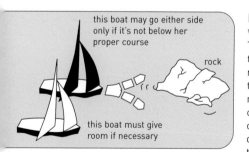

this boat may go either side only if it's not below her proper course

rock

this boat must give room if necessary

Room at an obstruction which is not continuing

The situation here is similar to the one when passing a mark (pages 53-57), but with the difference that the boat needing room can usually choose which side of the obstruction to go, and doesn't break a rule if she touches it.

Here White, without luffing rights, must not sail above her proper course and must give room to Black if she chooses to go to leeward of the rock and they are overlapped at two hull-lengths (rule 18.2(a)).

Luffing rights – two-boat situations

When boats become overlapped in any way other than the leeward boat establishing the overlap from clear astern within two lengths (laterally), the leeward boat has what is colloquially called 'luffing rights'. In other words, the right to sail above her proper course. A leeward boat with luffing rights may luff right up to head-to-wind (if she goes any further she will change tacks and no longer be the leeward boat).

However, there is one onerous restriction on the leeward boat: she must give room to the windward boat to keep clear. She may not luff so quickly that the windward boat is unable to respond to keep clear.

The windward boat must keep clear. In practice this means that whenever there are converging courses and a risk of collision, the windward boat must respond promptly by changing course so that they are no longer on a collision course.

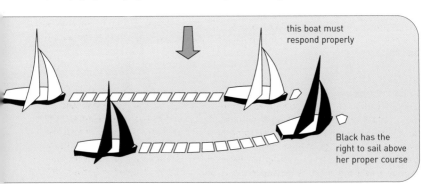

this boat must respond properly

Black has the right to sail above her proper course

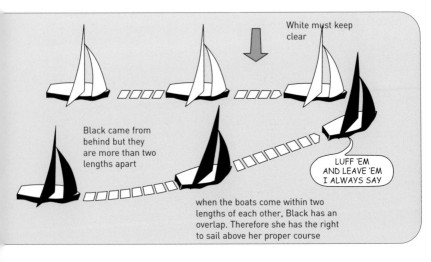

White must keep clear

Black came from behind but they are more than two lengths apart

LUFF 'EM AND LEAVE 'EM I ALWAYS SAY

when the boats come within two lengths of each other, Black has an overlap. Therefore she has the right to sail above her proper course

Here the black boat gybes, and becomes the right-of-way boat with luffing rights (the right to sail above her proper course). When she becomes the right-of-way boat, she must initially give White room to keep clear even if she doesn't change course, then she may luff but, if she does, she must give White room to keep clear (rules 15 and 16.1).

Luffing several boats

In the next picture, the first position shows L and I on opposite tacks. Boat I can sail any course but if she bears away she must give L room to keep clear, and of course Boat I is clear astern of W so must keep clear of her. L then gybes and since she did not establish the overlap on I from clear astern, L has luffing rights over I. L may sail higher than her proper course but must give room to I to keep clear. Now boat I gets an overlap to leeward of W. According to the definition of overlap (see page 21), L is overlapped to leeward of W too (since I is between W and L), and the overlap was established to leeward of W, so at the moment I is overlapped with W, L loses her luffing rights and must bear away to a course no higher than her proper course.

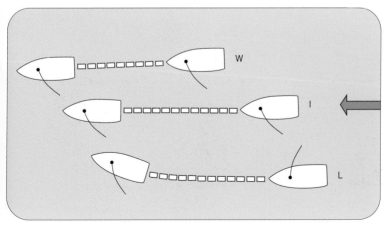

Stopping a luff

This sequence shows how a boat with luffing rights loses those rights. Soon after position 1, L and W become overlapped. As L didn't establish the overlap from clear astern L has luffing rights. W's wind-shadow affects L and W gains on L. At position 3, L luffs giving room to W to keep clear, and W responds. A sharp luff by W at position 4 breaks the overlap. L is now clear astern and becomes the keep-clear boat. W bears away and a new overlap is established. This time L establishes the overlap from clear astern so she doesn't have luffing rights, and she must sail no higher than her proper course. Her proper course is the course she would sail in the absence of W, starting from where she is at that moment, to finish as soon as possible. This means she will have to bear away at position 5. If she doesn't, W might want to protest, but she must still keep clear (rules 12, 11, 16 and 17.1).

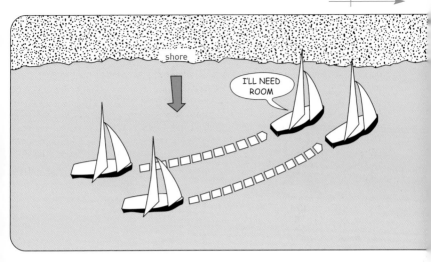

If the windward boat needs room because of a continuing obstruction such as the shore, then the leeward boat must give room. If there is something preventing the windward boat responding to the luff, then the leeward boat must not luff. There is no requirement for the inside boat to hail, but it's a good idea (rules 18.2(a), 18.5 and 16).

Sailing above a proper course

When two boats are overlapped, and the leeward boat established the overlap from clear astern and less than two lengths laterally, the leeward boat may not sail above her proper course while she remains overlapped within two lengths (rule 17.1).

But when the windward boat protests, claiming that the leeward boat is sailing above her proper course, the protest committee will not penalise the leeward boat unless it is satisfied the course was not a course that could reasonably be described as 'a course she would sail to finish as soon as possible in the absence of the windward boat' (definition of Proper Course and ISAF Case 14).

When the leeward boat has to gybe to fulfil her obligation not to sail above her proper course then she must gybe (rule 18.4).

When the leeward boat sails above her proper course, without the right to do so, the windward boat must still try to keep clear (rule 11).

GYBING

A boat that is gybing does not necessarily lose her rights
Gybing in itself places no additional obligations on a boat. Only when the right-of-way boat changes course must she give room to the keep-clear boat to keep clear (rule 16).

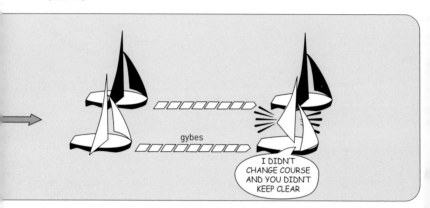

Before White gybes she is the leeward (right-of-way) boat. She may or may not have the right to sail above her proper course, depending on how the overlap was established. Without changing course she gybes on to starboard tack. At no time was she the keep-clear boat and she didn't change course, so if the booms touch, or White has to take action to prevent her boom making contact with Black's boom, then Black has broken rule 10 (the port-and-starboard rule) (rules 11 and 10).

Simultaneous gybing

When a boat gybes, she simply changes tack when the mainsail lies on the new side. If two boats gybe at the same time without changing course, the one that gybed on to port tack is wrong, because whether or not the other boat gybes, she gybes into a keep-clear position (rule 10).

THE
FINISH

The finish ends racing; it is also
the beginning of the protest
period – when this book may
again be useful.

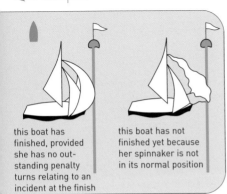

this boat has finished, provided she has no outstanding penalty turns relating to an incident at the finish

this boat has not finished yet because her spinnaker is not in its normal position

Finishing

A boat finishes when any part of her hull, crew or equipment in normal position, crosses the finishing line in the direction of the course from the last mark; either for the first time or, if she is taking a penalty (for hitting a finishing mark or breaking a 'when boats meet' rule, or after correcting an error made at the finishing line) (definition of Finishing).

A boat which has finished is still racing until she has cleared the finishing line, so a boat which breaks a rule before she has cleared the finish line, but after she has finished, must take her penalty for the infringement, and then finish again.

In the incident below, the port tack boat (white) would not have had to take a penalty if she had been clear of the finish line – that is, no longer intersecting any part of it – since she would not have been racing. But here she was still racing so she must sail clear, do a two-turns penalty, return to the pre-finish side of the line, and finish (rule 44.2).

To clear the finish line it is not necessary to sail right across it. The boat in the bottom picture has finished and cleared the line (definition of Finishing). (rule 28.1).

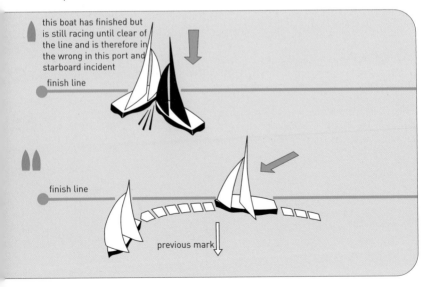

this boat has finished but is still racing until clear of the line and is therefore in the wrong in this port and starboard incident

finish line

finish line

previous mark

A boat also finishes correctly when capsized and the tide carries her across the finish line – provided all the crew are with the boat. But the crew may not swim the capsized boat to the finish line (rule 42).

Hitting a finishing mark

Hitting a finishing mark without having cleared the finish line is exonerated by sailing clear of other boats and doing a penalty turn, then returning to a position wholly on the course side of the finishing line, and finishing again. Obviously, the finishing position on the second crossing is the one that will be counted.

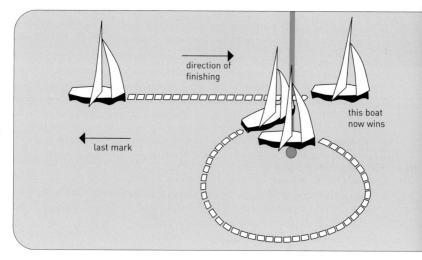

The 'hook finish'

A boat sailing a hook finish doesn't actually finish according to the definition, no matter what the sailing instructions say.

When a boat has crossed and cleared the finish line and sailed clear of the marks, but then drifts or sails back and hits a finishing mark, she is not penalised because she is no longer racing (definition of Racing and preamble to Part 2).

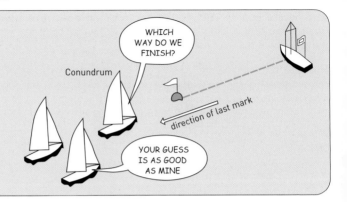

Conundrum will have difficulty knowing which way to finish on this badly set short-ened-course finishing line, and the race committee will have to count as finished all the boats, whichever way they cross. Some will have finished correctly (according to the definition) and the others will have to be given redress (by way of finishing places) for the error of the race committee in setting such an impossible finishing line.

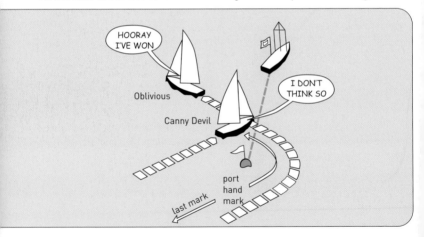

Canny Devil wins the race by being the first boat to finish in accordance with the def-inition (even if the sailing instructions said she must finish the way Oblivious did); Oblivious hasn't actually finished but she could unwind and finish correctly, or she might succeed in getting redress if she can convince a protest committee that the race committee confused her into thinking she was finishing correctly; but in giving redress, the protest committee cannot take away Canny Devil's victory.

OTHER IMPORTANT SAILING RULES, ENFORCEMENT AND PENALTIES

Competitive sailors are their own umpires. If we want our sport to stay healthy and enjoyable, every one of us has an interest in taking a penalty when we ourselves break a rule and protesting when someone else does and fails to take a penalty. Otherwise, anarchy ensues.

OTHER IMPORTANT SAILING RULES

Assisting a boat in distress
When in a position to do so, **every boat must help any boat or person in danger** (rule 1.1). You don't break a rule if you collide with another boat while trying to assist a boat or person in danger (rule 21). You can ask for redress to make up for any places you lose, but you can't get redress having lost places if the assistance is only to your own boat or your own crew (rule 62.1(c)).

Fair sailing
The fair sailing rule (rule 2) says boats must compete in 'compliance with recognised **principles of sportsmanship and fair play**'. Hailing 'starboard' when you're on port, with the intention of confusing a beginner is clearly unfair (ISAF Case 47). Interfering with a rival after the start when you know you are a premature starter, or leaning out further than normal to touch a windward boat, are other examples (ISAF Cases 65 and 73). Harassing another boat to hold her back other than for the reason of improving your own overall score is obviously unfair (ISAF Case 34).

Avoiding contact and damage
Every boat must avoid contact with other boats if reasonably possible, but only if there is damage can a right-of-way boat (or a boat entitled to room) be penalised (rule 14).

However, if you are the right-of-way boat, you don't have to start taking avoiding action until it is clear that the other boat is not keeping clear. If a port tack boat is bearing away under your stern, there is usually nothing you can do but hope she succeeds (rule 14(a)).

If you are the right-of-way boat and you have contact which was 'reasonably possible' to avoid, and there is damage but it's not serious, you can exonerate yourself by taking a two-turns penalty.

If it was 'reasonably possible' to avoid the contact, and the contact resulted in serious damage (to either boat, or even a third boat), whether the culprit was the keep-clear or the right-of-way boat you must retire (rule 44.1).

If you are the right-of-way boat and you have contact with another boat that you could have avoided, and there is no damage, you need not take a penalty (rule 14(b)).

Damage is anything a prudent owner would repair. Serious damage is damage that significantly affects the performance of the boat (or its crew), makes the boat unsafe, or is expensive to repair (ISAF Case 19).

Avoiding an anchored boat, or a boat capsized or aground
Other boats must, if possible, **avoid a boat that is anchored**. If you're anchored you must avoid other anchored boats (rule 21).

Anchoring includes lowering any weight to the bottom, or the crew standing on the bottom holding on to the boat. Anchoring does not mean tying up to or holding on to a mooring, moored boat or jetty. Neither does it mean standing on a jetty to hold the boat. None of these actions are allowed while you're racing, unless you are bailing out, reefing your sails, or making repairs (rule 45).

Other boats must, if possible, avoid a boat that is capsized or aground. For a boat to be 'capsized', it has to have its masthead in the water, so an upright swamped dinghy on port tack with no steerage way is a sitting duck. If it's not possible to avoid a capsized boat or a boat that has run aground, because it happens suddenly in front of you, then no rule is broken, even though there might be damage (rule 21).

Propulsion

There are some exceptions, but the basic rule says 'a boat shall compete by using only the wind and water to increase, maintain or decrease her speed. Her crew may adjust the trim of sails and hull, and perform other acts of seamanship, but shall not otherwise move their bodies to propel the boat' (rule 42.1).

In general terms, this means that the crew can move their body-weight to trim the boat, but not to impart energy into the boat to drive it forward. The sails can be moved to adjust for a change in wind strength or direction, but the move itself must not drive the boat forward.

There are some exceptions: you can propel your boat in any way you like if you are going to help someone in distress, or recovering a person overboard, or rendering assistance. Except on a beat, when surfing or planing conditions exist, you may pump (ie rapidly trim and release) any sail, or all sails, once, in order to initiate surfing or planing.

You can roll tack or gybe, provided that the manoeuvre doesn't mean you'd be going faster at the end of the tack or gybe than you would have been had you not tacked or gybed (rule 42.3(b)).

At well-organised regattas, a protest committee will be on the water and will protest competitors that it sees breaking the propulsion rule. Most competitors applaud such action, which if taken early in the series, inevitably results in suppressing the problem of competitors using 'kinetics' to increase their speed.

PENALTIES AND RULE ENFORCEMENT

Disqualification

A boat which is found by a protest committee to have broken a rule or a sailing instruction is usually disqualified from the race in which the infringement occurred. An exception is where a boat retires or does a **two-turns penalty promptly** after an incident in recognition that she has broken a rule, but also protests the other boat, claiming the other boat broke a rule; if the protest committee decides that she, the protesting boat, broke a rule, she will not be disqualified because she took a penalty.

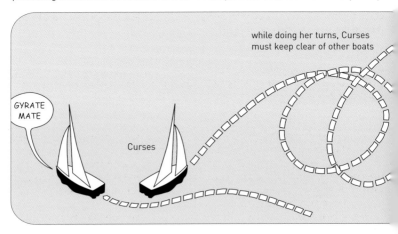

while doing her turns, Curses must keep clear of other boats

GYRATE MATE

Curses

A boat can exonerate herself for breaking a 'when boats meet' rule (those in Part 2 of the rules), by taking a two-turns penalty (rule 44.1). However, if she causes serious damage or gains a significant advantage in the race or series by her breach she must retire. A fundamental principle of sportsmanship is that when competitors break a rule they will promptly take a penalty (or retire) (rule: Sportsmanship and the Rules).

After getting well clear of other boats as soon after the incident as possible, a boat takes a two-turns penalty by promptly making two turns in the same direction, including two tacks and two gybes. When a boat takes the penalty at or near the finishing line, she must, after completing the penalty as soon as possible, sail completely to the course side of the line before finishing (rule 44.2).

The **penalty turns must be done at the first reasonable opportunity**. If the infringement was just before the mark, this might not be until the next leg, but you must actively find a clear enough patch of water to do the turns without getting in the way of other boats; you can't sail on, waiting for a space to appear.

While getting clear, a boat intending to take a penalty does not lose her rights, but while she is doing the turns she must keep clear (rule 20.2). A boat shall not change course if her only purpose is to interfere with a boat making a penalty turn or one on another leg or lap of the course.

Scoring penalty

The sailing instructions can annul the two-turns penalty system (in which case a boat infringing a rule must retire) or prescribe some other penalty system. The most common alternative to the two-turns penalty is the 'scoring penalty' (rule 44.3).

A boat takes a scoring penalty by displaying a yellow flag at the first reasonable opportunity after the incident, keeping it displayed until finishing, calling the race committee's attention to it at the finishing line, and informing the race committee of the identity of the other boat involved in the incident (rule 44.3).

The penalty is to make the boat's score worse than her actual finishing place by 20 per cent of the number of boats entered (unless the sailing instructions give some other number). The scores of other boats are not changed; therefore two boats may receive the same score (rule 44.3(c)).

Multiple penalties

A boat that takes a penalty is not penalised further with respect to the same incident unless she failed to retire when she caused serious damage or gained a significant advantage in the race or series (rules 44.4(b) and 44.1).

Touching a mark

After the preparatory signal, you mustn't let any part of your boat, equipment or crew touch a starting mark or a mark that begins, bounds or ends the leg of the course on which you are sailing, or a finishing mark after finishing but before clearing the line. However, if your boat does touch a mark, you may exonerate yourself by getting well clear of other boats as soon as possible, and taking a one-turn penalty: promptly making a turn including one tack and one gybe.

When a boat takes the penalty after touching a finishing mark, she must sail completely to the course side of the line before finishing (rule 31.2).

If a boat has gained a significant advantage in the race or series by touching the mark she must retire, even if by taking the penalty she ends up further back than she would be if she had not touched the mark (rule 31.2).

If a boat breaks a 'when boats meet rule' and touches a mark, provided she does not gain a significant advantage (or cause serious damage), she can exonerate herself with just one two-turn penalty (rule 44.1).

If a boat is wrongly compelled to touch a mark (for example when she should have been given room and wasn't), then she need not take a penalty (rules 31 and 64.1 (b)).

Even before the starting signal, a boat breaking a rule must do her turns as soon as possible. If the turns are not properly done and a valid protest is lodged, she will be disqualified.

When serious damage is caused, the boat in the wrong must retire; if she doesn't, she may be disqualified, even though she may have done her turns properly.

It is sometimes possible for a boat to deliberately break a rule, do the two-turns penalty and end up better off after the incident than she would have done by obeying the rules. A port tack boat rounding a windward mark, for example, against a strong tide in light air might lose less ground by refusing to give way to a starboard boat and take the penalty turns after rounding the mark than by tacking to keep clear of the starboard boat and failing to lay the mark, or ducking behind and losing a lot of ground. The port tack boat can be disqualified after a protest even though she might have done her turns immediately after the incident (rule 44.1).

Protest by one competitor against another

If you make contact with another boat and you don't think you have broken a rule, and the other boat doesn't take a penalty, you don't have to protest. Even if you hail 'protest', you don't have to go through with it. Even if it is lodged in writing, a protestor may ask for it to be withdrawn, and this will usually be allowed.

When a 'third boat' which witnesses, but is not involved in, an incident wants to protest, she must hail 'protest', or if the protested boat is too far away, inform her as soon as possible. If the third boat's protest is valid, it must be heard by the protest committee. If the protest was against the wrong boat, or quoted the wrong rule, the boat that broke a rule can still be penalised.

When you are involved in an incident in which another boat has broken a rule, or when you are not involved but see what you think is a boat breaking a rule, and not taking a penalty, you are entitled to protest (rule 60.1). A protest is decided ashore by a protest committee, which is usually a committee appointed by the race committee. It acts rather like a court of law, first hearing the evidence and then giving its verdict as to which, if any, boat (or boats) has broken a rule. Those it decides have broken a rule are disqualified.

A helmsman who decides to protest must hail 'protest' (and, if the boat's hull length is six metres or more, display a protest flag) (rule 61.1(a)).

If you see a boat breaking a rule, but you are not involved in the incident, and you want to protest, you must hail 'protest'. If you hear that one of the boats involved is going to protest, especially if you hear him shouting 'protest', remember he might not actually lodge the protest, and if you haven't hailed, then your protest would be ruled as invalid.

On coming ashore, the boat protesting must put in a written protest to the race committee (rule 61.2). The protest must be delivered within two hours of the time the last boat finishes (unless the sailing instructions specify some different time or the protest committee has reason to extend the time), but when there is a good reason to do so, the protest committee must extend the time limit (rule 61.3).

The protestee (the representative of the protested boat) is entitled to a copy of the protest, or if that's not possible, then time to study the original. The protestee must make a reasonable attempt to find out when the protest is to be heard, and make himself available for the hearing.

Protest by a race committee or protest committee

Having seen what it thinks is a boat breaking a rule and not taking a penalty, the race committee (or the protest committee, if there is one) may protest. It obviously doesn't have to display a flag, and it doesn't have to inform the boat until after the race – too late for the boat to take a penalty (rule 61.1(b)). For what incidents should the race committee (or protest committee) protest? In my opinion, only when it sees the sort of infringement which has the effect of gaining on the rest of the fleet (like breaking the propulsion rule) rather than just the other boat involved, or where there is a gross infringement, or damage.

If the race committee believes you haven't started or finished, it can score you as DNS or DNF without a hearing. If you think the committee has made a mistake, it's best just to ask first. If the race committee doesn't fix the error (or satisfy you that it was correct) then you can ask for redress, and get a formal hearing. You should make your request in writing as soon as you can.

Disqualification without a hearing

Unless the sailing instructions have extended the power of the race committee or the protest committee to disqualify a boat without a hearing (which is often the case in major championships for infringements of rule 42 (Propulsion)), the only infringements for which a race committee may penalise a boat without a hearing are failing to start or finish correctly. (They are scored 'DNS' for 'did not start', 'OCS' for 'on the course side' of the starting line at the start, or 'DNF' for 'did not finish'.) A competitor who doesn't agree can ask for redress, but it's best to ask the race officer first (rule 60.1(b)).

Requesting redress

When a competitor believes his finishing position has been prejudiced by an improper act or omission of the race committee, he may make a 'request for redress' (rules 60.1(b) and 62.1(a)).

The request must be in writing and be received within the time limit for protests or within two hours of the incident (which, if it's something to do with scoring, might be after the race when the results get posted) (rule 62.2).

The protest committee must proceed with a hearing, but before even considering what redress is appropriate, it must be satisfied that the boat's finishing position in the race (or series) has been made significantly worse, and that this was through no fault of the boat. It must also be satisfied that it was due to an improper act or omission of the race committee (or one of the other reasons that allows redress to be given) (rule 62.1). If these criteria are met, it must give redress, but giving redress means making as fair an arrangement as possible for all boats affected, not just the one asking for redress. Sometimes this means letting the results stand. Usually it means adjusting the points for the boat asking for redress. Very rarely is cancelling the race the best solution (rule 64.2).

Redress can also be given when a boat gives assistance to someone in distress while racing, being physically damaged by a boat breaking a 'when boats meet' rule, or being disadvantaged by a boat which is found to have broken the fair sailing rule or found guilty of 'gross misconduct' (rules 62.1 and 69.1).

Composition of a protest committee

At a local or club event, the protest committee is appointed by the race committee. No one may be on a protest committee who might benefit from that committee's decision. Interpreted strictly, this would bar competitors from protest committees, but in practice competitors can be included provided both protestor and defendant agree. So at the start of the hearing, the protestor and defendant should be asked whether they object to any member of the protest committee, those members who competed in the race or the series being pointed out. If there are no objections, then an appeal solely on the grounds that a member of the protest committee was an 'interested party' would not succeed (rule 63.4).

At major events, the organising authority appoints a protest committee which is independent of the race committee; its decisions are usually open to appeal (even by the race committee if it doesn't agree with a decision to which it was a party) (rule 70.1).

The right to appeal

The decision of a protest committee or jury can usually be referred to the national authority in whose jurisdiction the event was held. The national authority's decision is final. The International Sailing Federation does not decide appeals. However, an appeal to the national authority can be considered only on a question of rule interpretation, not on a question of fact. The final arbiter of fact is the protest committee (rule 70.1).

For some major events like World Championships an International Jury is appointed; then there is no right of appeal. The waiving of the right to appeal is also common in two-day team racing events where teams must be eliminated from early rounds before there can be a final. An appeal of a decision in all but the final round would dislocate the whole event. Under these circumstances, the organisers can deny the right of appeal. In some countries, permission from the national authority is required, which is given when the NA approves the membership of the jury.

There is no right of appeal against a decision by an International Jury acting in accordance with Appendix N.

Counter-protest

It often happens that both boats involved in an incident lodge a protest, or one of the two involved protests and a boat not involved also protests. The validity of each protest is considered separately, and if both or all protests are valid, they are heard simultaneously if they are about the same incident, or even two closely related incidents. If one protest is found not to be valid (perhaps there was no hail) then of course it makes little difference because the other protest will be heard (ISAF Case 49).

The protest hearing

The procedure for hearing a protest is well explained in Appendix M of the rules. It is important that this is followed carefully, as major errors of procedure can result in decisions being changed on appeal. If any of the 'parties' (protestor or protestee) feel that procedural errors are being made, the issue should be raised at the time. Failure to complain at the time, or as soon as the wrong procedure became known, would mean that an appeal based on the procedural errors would be dismissed.

The defendant and the protestor have the right to be present at the hearing and throughout the taking of evidence (rule 63.3(a)). When either the defendant or protestor has made a reasonable attempt to be present he should be allowed to be present. So if a committee has several protests to hear, it should hear those where both parties are present first. But if an interested party fails to make an effort to attend the hearing, the protest committee may deal with the case in his absence (rule 63.3(b)).

The protestor and defendant may call as many witnesses as they choose, and every witness may be questioned by the committee and the other party. The protest committee will deliberate in private, and then recall the parties to announce its decision. This is in the form of 'facts found' (what it thinks happened), the 'decision' (whether a boat is to be penalised, and if so which one(s)), the 'grounds for the decision' and the rule numbers that apply. Any party can get a written copy if they ask for it in writing within seven days (rule 65.2).

THE RACING RULES OF SAILING

2005~2008 rules

CONTENTS

INTRODUCTION

The Racing Rules of Sailing includes two main sections. The first, Parts 1–7, contains rules that affect all competitors. The second, Appendices A–P, provides details of rules, rules that apply to particular kinds of racing, and rules that affect only a small number of competitors or officials.

Revision   The racing rules are revised and published every four years by the International Sailing Federation (ISAF), the international authority for the sport. This edition becomes effective on 1 January 2005. Marginal markings indicate important changes to Parts 1–7 and the Definitions of the 2001–2004 edition. No changes are contemplated before 2009, but any changes determined to be urgent before then will be announced through national authorities and posted on the ISAF website (www.sailing.org).

ISAF Codes   The ISAF Eligibility, Advertising and Anti-Doping Codes (Regulations 19, 20 and 21) are referred to in the definition *Rule* but are not included in this book because they can be changed at any time. New versions will be announced through national authorities and posted on the ISAF website.

Cases and Calls   The ISAF publishes interpretations of the racing rules in *The Case Book for 2005–2008* and recognizes them as authoritative interpretations and explanations of the rules. It also publishes *The Call Book for Match Racing for 2005–2008* and *The Call Book for Team Racing for 2005–2008*, and it recognizes them as authoritative only for umpired match or team racing. These publications are available on the ISAF website.

Terminology   A term used in the sense stated in the Definitions is printed in italics or, in preambles, in bold italics (for example, *racing* and **racing**). 'Boat' means a sailboat and the crew on board. 'Race committee' includes any person or committee performing a race committee function. Other words and terms are used in the sense ordinarily understood in nautical or general use.

Appendices   When the rules of an appendix apply, they take precedence over any conflicting rules in Parts 1–7. Each appendix is identified by a letter. A reference to a rule in an appendix will contain the letter and the rule number (for example, 'rule A1'). There is no Appendix I or O.

Changes to the Rules   The prescriptions of a national authority, class rules or the sailing instructions may change a racing rule only as permitted in rule 86.

Changes to National Authority Prescriptions   A national authority may restrict changes to its prescriptions as provided in rule 87.

BASIC PRINCIPLE

SPORTSMANSHIP AND THE RULES
Competitors in the sport of sailing are governed by a body of *rules* that they are expected to follow and enforce. A fundamental principle of sportsmanship is that when competitors break a *rule* they will promptly take a penalty, which may be to retire.

PART 1 – FUNDAMENTAL RULES

1   **SAFETY**

1.1   **Helping Those in Danger**

A boat or competitor shall give all possible help to any person or vessel in danger.

1.2   **Life-Saving Equipment and Personal Buoyancy**

A boat shall carry adequate life-saving equipment for all persons on board, including one item ready for immediate use, unless her class rules make some other provision. Each competitor is individually responsible for wearing personal buoyancy adequate for the conditions.

2   **FAIR SAILING**

A boat and her owner shall compete in compliance with recognized principles of sportsmanship and fair play. A boat may be penalized under this rule only if it is clearly established that these principles have been violated. A disqualification under this rule shall not be excluded from the boat's series score.

3   ACCEPTANCE OF THE RULES
By participating in a race conducted under these racing rules, each competitor and boat owner agrees:
(a) to be governed by the *rules*;
(b) to accept the penalties imposed and other action taken under the *rules*, subject to the appeal and review procedures provided in them, as the final determination of any matter arising under the *rules*; and
(c) with respect to such determination, not to resort to any court or other tribunal not provided in the *rules*.

4   DECISION TO RACE
The responsibility for a boat's decision to participate in a race or to continue *racing* is hers alone.

5   BANNED SUBSTANCES AND METHODS
A competitor shall neither take a substance nor use a method banned by the Olympic Movement Anti-Doping Code or the World Anti-Doping Agency and shall comply with ISAF Regulation 21, Anti-Doping Code. An alleged or actual breach of this rule shall be dealt with under Regulation 21. It shall not be grounds for a *protest* and rule 63.1 does not apply.

PART 2 – WHEN BOATS MEET

The rules of Part 2 apply between boats that are sailing in or near the racing area and intend to **race***, are* **racing***, or have been* **racing***. However, a boat not* **racing** *shall not be penalized for breaking one of these rules, except rule 22.1. When a boat sailing under these rules meets a vessel that is not, she shall comply with the International Regulations for Preventing Collisions at Sea (IRPCAS) or government right-of-way rules. However, an alleged breach of those rules shall not be grounds for a* **protest** *except by the race committee or protest committee. If the sailing instructions so state, the rules of Part 2 are replaced by the right-of-way rules of the IRPCAS or by government right-of-way rules.*

Section A – Right of Way

*A boat has right of way when another boat is required to **keep clear** of her. However, some rules in Sections B, C and D limit the actions of a right-of-way boat.*

10   ON OPPOSITE TACKS

When boats are on opposite *tacks*, a *port-tack* boat shall keep *clear* of a *starboard-tack* boat.

11   ON THE SAME TACK, OVERLAPPED

When boats are on the same *tack* and *overlapped*, a *windward* boat shall *keep clear* of a *leeward* boat.

12   ON THE SAME TACK, NOT OVERLAPPED

When boats are on the same *tack* and not *overlapped*, a boat *clear astern* shall *keep clear* of a boat *clear ahead*.

13   WHILE TACKING

After a boat passes head to wind, she shall *keep clear* of other boats until she is on a close-hauled course. During that time rules 10, 11 and 12 do not apply. If two boats are subject to this rule at the same time, the one on the other's port side or the one astern shall *keep clear*.

Section B – General Limitations

14   AVOIDING CONTACT

A boat shall avoid contact with another boat if reasonably possible. However, a right-of-way boat or one entitled to *room*

(a)   need not act to avoid contact until it is clear that the other boat is not *keeping clear* or giving *room*, and

(b)   shall not be penalized under this rule unless there is contact that causes damage or injury.

15   ACQUIRING RIGHT OF WAY

When a boat acquires right of way, she shall initially give the other boat *room* to *keep clear*, unless she acquires right of way because of the other boat's actions.

16   CHANGING COURSE

16.1   When a right-of-way boat changes course, she shall give the other boat *room* to *keep clear*.

16.2   In addition, when after the starting signal a *port-tack* boat is *keeping clear* by sailing to pass astern of a *starboard-tack* boat, the *starboard-tack* boat shall not change course if as a result the *port-tack* boat would immediately need to change course to continue *keeping clear*.

17   ON THE SAME TACK; PROPER COURSE

17.1   If a boat *clear astern* becomes *overlapped* within two of her hull lengths to *leeward* of a boat on the same *tack*, she shall not sail above her *proper course* while they remain *overlapped* within that distance, unless in doing so she promptly sails astern of the other boat. This rule does not apply if the *overlap* begins while the *windward* boat is required by rule 13 to *keep clear*.

17.2   Except on a beat to windward, while a boat is less than two of her hull lengths from a *leeward* boat or a boat *clear astern* steering a course to *leeward* of her, she shall not sail below her *proper course* unless she gybes.

Section C – At Marks and Obstructions

To the extent that a Section C rule conflicts with a rule in Section A or B, the Section C rule takes precedence.

18   ROUNDING AND PASSING MARKS AND OBSTRUCTIONS
*In rule 18, **room** is **room** for an inside boat to round or pass between an outside boat and a **mark** or **obstruction**, including **room** to tack or gybe when either is a normal part of the manoeuvre.*

18.1   **When This Rule Applies**
Rule 18 applies when boats are about to round or pass a *mark* they are required to leave on the same side, or an *obstruction* on the same side, until they have passed it. However, it does not apply

(a)   at a starting *mark* surrounded by navigable water or at its anchor line from the time the boats are approaching them to *start* until they have passed them, or

(b)   while the boats are on opposite *tacks*, either on a beat to windward or when the *proper course* for one of them, but not both, to round or pass the *mark* or *obstruction* is to tack.

18.2 **Giving Room; Keeping Clear**

(a) OVERLAPPED – BASIC RULE

When boats are *overlapped* the outside boat shall give the inside boat *room* to round or pass the *mark* or *obstruction*, and if the inside boat has right of way the outside boat shall also *keep clear*. Other parts of rule 18 contain exceptions to this rule.

(b) OVERLAPPED AT THE ZONE

If boats were *overlapped* before either of them reached the *two-length zone* and the *overlap* is broken after one of them has reached it, the boat that was on the outside shall continue to give the other boat *room*. If the outside boat becomes *clear astern* or *overlapped* inside the other boat, she is not entitled to *room* and shall *keep clear*.

(c) NOT OVERLAPPED AT THE ZONE

If a boat was *clear ahead* at the time she reached the *two-length zone*, the boat *clear astern* shall thereafter *keep clear*. If the boat *clear astern* becomes *overlapped* outside the other boat, she shall also give the inside boat *room*. If the boat *clear astern* becomes *overlapped* inside the other boat, she is not entitled to *room*. If the boat that was *clear ahead* passes head to wind, rule 18.2(c) no longer applies and remains inapplicable.

(d) CHANGING COURSE TO ROUND OR PASS

When after the starting signal rule 18 applies between two boats and the right-of-way boat is changing course to round or pass a *mark*, rule 16 does not apply between her and the other boat.

(e) OVERLAP RIGHTS

If there is reasonable doubt that a boat obtained or broke an *overlap* in time, it shall be presumed that she did not. If the outside boat is unable to give *room* when an *overlap* begins, rules 18.2(a) and 18.2(b) do not apply.

18.3 **Tacking at a Mark**

If two boats were approaching a *mark* on opposite *tacks* and one of them completes a tack in the *two-length zone* when the other is fetching the *mark*, rule 18.2 does not apply. The boat that tacked

(a) shall not cause the other boat to sail above close-hauled to avoid her or prevent the other boat from passing the *mark*, and

(b) shall give *room* if the other boat becomes *overlapped* inside her, in which case rule 15 does not apply.

18.4   Gybing

When an inside *overlapped* right-of-way boat must gybe at a *mark* or *obstruction* to sail her *proper course*, until she gybes she shall sail no farther from the *mark* or *obstruction* than needed to sail that course.

18.5   Passing a Continuing Obstruction

While boats are passing a continuing *obstruction*, rules 18.2(b) and 18.2(c) do not apply. A boat *clear astern* that obtains an inside *overlap* is entitled to *room* to pass between the other boat and the *obstruction* only if at the moment the *overlap* begins there is *room* to do so. If there is not, she is not entitled to *room* and shall *keep clear*.

19   ROOM TO TACK AT AN OBSTRUCTION

19.1   When approaching an *obstruction*, a boat sailing close-hauled or above may hail for *room* to tack and avoid another boat on the same *tack*. However, she shall not hail unless safety requires her to make a substantial course change to avoid the *obstruction*. Before tacking she shall give the hailed boat time to respond. The hailed boat shall respond by either

(a) tacking as soon as possible, in which case the hailing boat shall also tack as soon as possible, or

(b) immediately replying 'You tack', in which case the hailing boat shall tack as soon as possible and the hailed boat shall give *room*, and rules 10 and 13 do not apply.

19.2   Rule 19.1 does not apply at a starting *mark* surrounded by navigable water or at its anchor line from the time boats are approaching them to *start* until they have passed them or at a *mark* that the hailed boat can fetch. When rule 19.1 applies, rule 18 does not.

Section D – Other Rules

When rule 20 or 21 applies between two boats, Section A rules do not.

20   STARTING ERRORS; PENALTY TURNS; MOVING ASTERN

20.1   A boat sailing towards the pre-start side of the starting line or its extensions after her starting signal to *start* or to comply with rule 30.1 shall *keep clear* of a boat not doing so until she is completely on the pre-start side.

20.2   A boat making a penalty turn shall *keep clear* of one that is not.

20.3   A boat moving astern by backing a sail shall *keep clear* of one that is not.

21   CAPSIZED, ANCHORED OR AGROUND; RESCUING
       If possible, a boat shall avoid a boat that is capsized or has not regained control after capsizing, is anchored or aground, or is trying to help a person or vessel in danger. A boat is capsized when her masthead is in the water.

22   INTERFERING WITH ANOTHER BOAT

22.1   If reasonably possible, a boat not *racing* shall not interfere with a boat that is *racing*.

22.2   A boat shall not change course if her only purpose is to interfere with a boat making a penalty turn or one on another leg or lap of the course.

PART 3 – CONDUCT OF A RACE

25   NOTICE OF RACE, SAILING INSTRUCTIONS AND SIGNALS
       The notice of race and sailing instructions shall be made available to each boat before a race begins. The meanings of the visual and sound signals stated in Race Signals shall not be changed except under rule 86.1(b). The meanings of any other signals that may be used shall be stated in the sailing instructions.

26   STARTING RACES
       Races shall be started by using the following signals. Times shall be taken from the visual signals; the absence of a sound signal shall be disregarded.

Signal	Flag and sound	Minutes before starting signal
Warning	Class flag; 1 sound	5*
Preparatory	P, I, Z, Z with I, or black flag; 1 sound	4
One-minute	Preparatory flag removed; 1 long sound	1
Starting	Class flag removed; 1 sound	0

*or as stated in the sailing instructions

The warning signal for each succeeding class shall be made with or after the starting signal of the preceding class.

27 OTHER RACE COMMITTEE ACTIONS BEFORE THE STARTING SIGNAL

27.1 No later than the warning signal, the race committee shall signal or otherwise designate the course to be sailed if the sailing instructions have not stated the course, and it may replace one course signal with another and signal that wearing personal buoyancy is required (display flag Y with one sound).

27.2 No later than the preparatory signal, the race committee may move a starting *mark* and may apply rule 30.

27.3 Before the starting signal, the race committee may for any reason *postpone* (display flag AP, AP over H, or AP over A, with two sounds) or *abandon* the race (display flag N over H, or N over A, with three sounds).

28 SAILING THE COURSE

28.1 A boat shall *start*, leave each *mark* on the required side in the correct order, and *finish*, so that a string representing her wake after *starting* and until *finishing* would when drawn taut pass each *mark* on the required side and touch each rounding *mark*. She may correct any errors to comply with this rule. After *finishing* she need not cross the finishing line completely.

28.2 A boat may leave on either side a *mark* that does not begin, bound or end the leg she is on. However, she shall leave a starting *mark* on the required side when she is approaching the starting line from its pre-start side to *start*.

29   RECALLS

29.1   Individual Recall

When at a boat's starting signal any part of her hull, crew or equipment is on the course side of the starting line or she must comply with rule 30.1, the race committee shall promptly display flag X with one sound. The flag shall be displayed until all such boats are completely on the pre-start side of the starting line or its extensions and have complied with rule 30.1 if it applies, but not later than four minutes after the starting signal or one minute before any later starting signal, whichever is earlier.

29.2   General Recall

When at the starting signal the race committee is unable to identify boats that are on the course side of the starting line or to which rule 30 applies, or there has been an error in the starting procedure, the race committee may signal a general recall (display the First Substitute with 2 sounds). The warning signal for a new start for the recalled class shall be made one minute after the First Substitute is removed (one sound), and starts for any succeeding classes shall follow the new start.

30   STARTING PENALTIES

30.1   Round-an-End Rule

If flag I has been displayed, and any part of a boat's hull, crew or equipment is on the course side of the starting line or its extensions during the minute before her starting signal, she shall thereafter sail from the course side across an extension to the pre-start side before *starting*.

30.2   20% Penalty Rule

If flag Z has been displayed, no part of a boat's hull, crew or equipment shall be in the triangle formed by the ends of the starting line and the first *mark* during the minute before her starting signal. If a boat breaks this rule and is identified, she shall receive, without a hearing, a 20% scoring penalty calculated as stated in rule 44.3(c). She shall be penalized even if the race is restarted, resailed or rescheduled, but not if it is *postponed* or *abandoned* before the starting signal.

30.3   Black Flag Rule

If a black flag has been displayed, no part of a boat's hull, crew or equipment shall be in the triangle formed by the ends of the starting line and the first *mark* during the minute before her starting signal. If a boat breaks this rule and is identified, she shall be disqualified without a hearing, even if the race is restarted, resailed or rescheduled, but not if it is *postponed* or *abandoned* before the starting signal. If a general recall is signalled or the race is *abandoned* after the starting signal, the race committee shall display her sail number before the next warning signal for that race, and if the race is restarted or resailed she shall not sail in it. If she does so, her disqualification shall not be excluded in calculating her series score.

If this rule applies rule 29.1 does not.

31   TOUCHING A MARK

31.1   While *racing*, a boat shall not touch a starting *mark* before *starting*, a *mark* that begins, bounds or ends the leg of the course on which she is sailing, or a finishing *mark* after *finishing*.

31.2   A boat that has broken rule 31.1 may, after getting well clear of other boats as soon as possible, take a penalty by promptly making one turn including one tack and one gybe. When a boat takes the penalty after touching a finishing *mark*, she shall sail completely to the course side of the line before *finishing*. However, if a boat has gained a significant advantage in the race or series by touching the *mark* her penalty shall be to retire.

32   SHORTENING OR ABANDONING AFTER THE START

32.1   After the starting signal, the race committee may shorten the course (display flag S with two sounds) or *abandon* the race (display flag N, N over H, or N over A, with three sounds), as appropriate,

(a) because of an error in the starting procedure,
(b) because of foul weather,
(c) because of insufficient wind making it unlikely that any boat will *finish* within the time limit,
(d) because a *mark* is missing or out of position, or
(e) for any other reason directly affecting the safety or fairness of the competition,

or may shorten the course so that other scheduled races can be sailed. However, after one boat has sailed the course and *finished* within the time limit, if any, the race committee shall not *abandon* the race without considering the consequences for all boats in the race or series.

32.2   If the race committee signals a shortened course (displays flag S with two sounds), the finishing line shall be,

(a)   at a rounding *mark*, between the *mark* and a staff displaying flag S;

(b)   at a line boats are required to cross at the end of each lap, that line;

(c)   at a gate, between the gate *marks*.

33   **CHANGING THE NEXT LEG OF THE COURSE**
The race committee may change a leg of the course that begins at a rounding *mark* by changing the position of the next *mark* (or finish line) and signalling all boats before they begin the leg. The next *mark* need not be in position at that time.

(a)   If the direction of the leg will be changed, the signal shall be the display of flag C with repetitive sounds and either

(1)   the new compass bearing or

(2)   a green triangular flag or board for a change to starboard or a red rectangular flag or board for a change to port.

(b)   If the length of the leg will be changed, the signal shall be the display of flag C with repetitive sounds and a '–' if the leg will be shortened or a '+' if the leg will be lengthened.

(c)   Subsequent legs may be changed without further signalling to maintain the course shape.

34   **MARK MISSING**
If a *mark* is missing or out of position, the race committee shall, if possible,

(a)   replace it in its correct position or substitute a new one of similar appearance, or

(b)   substitute an object displaying flag M and make repetitive sound signals.

35   **TIME LIMIT AND SCORES**
If one boat sails the course as required by rule 28.1 and *finishes* within the time limit, if any, all boats that *finish* shall be scored according to their finishing places unless the race is *abandoned*. If no boat *finishes* within the time limit, the race committee shall *abandon* the race.

36   RACES RESTARTED OR RESAILED

If a race is restarted or resailed, a breach of a *rule*, other than rule 30.3, in the original race shall not prohibit a boat from competing or, except under rule 30.2, 30.3 or 69, cause her to be penalized.

PART 4 – OTHER REQUIREMENTS WHEN RACING

Part 4 rules apply only to boats **racing**.

40   PERSONAL BUOYANCY; HARNESSES

40.1   When flag Y is displayed with one sound before or with the warning signal, competitors shall wear life-jackets or other adequate personal buoyancy. Wet suits and dry suits are not adequate personal buoyancy.

40.2   A trapeze or hiking harness shall have a device that can quickly release the competitor from the boat at any time while in use. *Note: This rule takes effect on 1 January 2006.*

41   OUTSIDE HELP

A boat shall not receive help from any outside source, except

(a)   help as provided for in rule 1;

(b)   help for an ill or injured crew member;

(c)   after a collision, help from the crew of the other boat to get clear;

(d)   help in the form of information freely available to all boats;

(e)   unsolicited information from a disinterested source, which may be another boat in the same race.

42   PROPULSION

42.1   **Basic Rule**

Except when permitted in rule 42.3 or 45, a boat shall compete by using only the wind and water to increase, maintain or decrease her speed. Her crew may adjust the trim of sails and hull, and perform other acts of seamanship, but shall not otherwise move their bodies to propel the boat.

42.2   Prohibited Actions
Without limiting the application of rule 42.1, these actions are prohibited:

(a)   pumping: repeated fanning of any sail either by pulling in and releasing the sail or by vertical or athwartships body movement;

(b)   rocking: repeated rolling of the boat, induced by
    (1)   body movement,
    (2)   repeated adjustment of the sails or centreboard, or
    (3)   steering;

(c)   ooching: sudden forward body movement, stopped abruptly;

(d)   sculling: repeated movement of the helm that is either forceful or that propels the boat forward or prevents her from moving astern;

(e)   repeated tacks or gybes unrelated to changes in the wind or to tactical considerations.

42.3   Exceptions
(a)   A boat may be rolled to facilitate steering.

(b)   A boat's crew may move their bodies to exaggerate the rolling that facilitates steering the boat through a tack or a gybe, provided that, just after the tack or gybe is completed, the boat's speed is not greater than it would have been in the absence of the tack or gybe.

(c)   Except on a beat to windward, when surfing (rapidly accelerating down the leeward side of a wave) or planing is possible, the boat's crew may pull the sheet and the guy controlling any sail in order to initiate surfing or planing, but only once for each wave or gust of wind.

(d)   When a boat is above a close-hauled course and either stationary or moving slowly, she may scull to turn to a close-hauled course.

(e)   A boat may reduce speed by repeatedly moving her helm.

(f)   Any means of propulsion may be used to help a person or another vessel in danger.

(g) To get clear after grounding or colliding with another boat or object, a boat may use force applied by the crew of either boat and any equipment other than a propulsion engine.

Note: Interpretations of rule 42 are available at the ISAF website (www.sailing.org) or by mail upon request.

43   COMPETITOR CLOTHING AND EQUIPMENT

43.1   (a) Competitors shall not wear or carry clothing or equipment for the purpose of increasing their weight.

(b) Furthermore, a competitor's clothing and equipment shall not weigh more than 8 kilograms, excluding a hiking or trapeze harness and clothing (including footwear) worn only below the knee. Class rules or sailing instructions may specify a lower weight or a higher weight up to 10 kilograms. Class rules may include footwear and other clothing worn below the knee within that weight. A hiking or trapeze harness shall have positive buoyancy and shall not weigh more than 2 kilograms, except that class rules may specify a higher weight up to 4 kilograms. Weights shall be determined as required by Appendix H.

(c) When a measurer in charge of weighing clothing and equipment believes a competitor may have broken rule 43.1(a) or 43.1(b) he shall report the matter in writing to the race committee, which shall protest the boat of the competitor.

43.2   Rule 43.1(b) does not apply to boats required to be equipped with lifelines.

44   PENALTIES FOR BREAKING RULES OF PART 2

44.1   Taking a Penalty
A boat that may have broken a rule of Part 2 while *racing* may take a penalty at the time of the incident. Her penalty shall be a Two-Turns Penalty unless the sailing instructions specify the use of the Scoring Penalty or some other penalty. However, if she caused injury or serious damage or gained a significant advantage in the race or series by her breach her penalty shall be to retire.

44.2   Two-Turns Penalty
After getting well clear of other boats as soon after the incident as possible, a boat takes a Two-Turns Penalty by promptly mak-

ing two turns in the same direction, including two tacks and two gybes. When a boat takes the penalty at or near the finishing line, she shall sail completely to the course side of the line before *finishing*.

44.3   Scoring Penalty

(a)   A boat takes a Scoring Penalty by displaying a yellow flag at the first reasonable opportunity after the incident, keeping it displayed until *finishing*, and calling the race committee's attention to it at the finishing line. At that time she shall also inform the race committee of the identity of the other boat involved in the incident. If this is impracticable, she shall do so at the first reasonable opportunity within the time limit for *protests*.

(b)   If a boat displays a yellow flag, she shall also comply with the other parts of rule 44.3(a).

(c)   The boat's penalty score shall be the score for the place worse than her actual finishing place by the number of places stated in the sailing instructions, except that she shall not be scored worse than Did Not Finish. When the sailing instructions do not state the number of places, the number shall be the whole number (rounding 0.5 upward) nearest to 20% of the number of boats entered. The scores of other boats shall not be changed; therefore, two boats may receive the same score.

44.4   Limits on Penalties

(a)   When a boat intends to take a penalty as provided in rule 44.1 and in the same incident has touched a *mark*, she need not take the penalty provided in rule 31.2.

(b)   A boat that takes a penalty shall not be penalized further with respect to the same incident unless she failed to retire when rule 44.1 required her to do so.

45   HAULING OUT; MAKING FAST; ANCHORING

A boat shall be afloat and off moorings at her preparatory signal. Thereafter, she shall not be hauled out or made fast except to bail out, reef sails or make repairs. She may anchor or the crew may stand on the bottom. She shall recover the anchor before continuing in the race unless she is unable to do so.

46   PERSON IN CHARGE

A boat shall have on board a person in charge designated by the member or organization that entered the boat. See rule 75.

47   **LIMITATIONS ON EQUIPMENT AND CREW**

47.1   A boat shall use only the equipment on board at her preparatory signal.

47.2   No person on board shall intentionally leave, except when ill or injured, or to help a person or vessel in danger, or to swim. A person leaving the boat by accident or to swim shall be back on board before the boat continues in the race.

48   **FOG SIGNALS AND LIGHTS**
When safety requires, a boat shall sound fog signals and show lights as required by the *International Regulations for Preventing Collisions at Sea* or applicable government rules.

49   **CREW POSITION**

49.1   Competitors shall use no device designed to position their bodies outboard, other than hiking straps and stiffeners worn under the thighs.

49.2   When lifelines are required by the class rules or the sailing instructions they shall be taut, and competitors shall not position any part of their torsos outside them, except briefly to perform a necessary task. On boats equipped with upper and lower lifelines of wire, a competitor sitting on the deck facing outboard with his waist inside the lower lifeline may have the upper part of his body outside the upper lifeline.

50   **SETTING AND SHEETING SAILS**

50.1   **Changing Sails**
When headsails or spinnakers are being changed, a replacing sail may be fully set and trimmed before the replaced sail is lowered. However, only one mainsail and, except when changing, only one spinnaker shall be carried set at a time.

50.2   **Spinnaker Poles; Whisker Poles**
Only one spinnaker pole or whisker pole shall be used at a time except when gybing. When in use, it shall be attached to the foremost mast.

50.3   **Use of Outriggers**
(a)   No sail shall be sheeted over or through an outrigger, except as permitted in rule 50.3(b) or 50.3(c). An outrigger is any

fitting or other device so placed that it could exert outward pressure on a sheet or sail at a point from which, with the boat upright, a vertical line would fall out-side the hull or deck planking. For the purpose of this rule, bulwarks, rails and rubbing strakes are not part of the hull or deck planking and the following are not outriggers: a bowsprit used to secure the tack of a working sail, a bumkin used to sheet the boom of a working sail, or a boom of a boomed headsail that requires no adjustment when tacking.

(b) Any sail may be sheeted to or led above a boom that is regularly used for a working sail and is permanently attached to the mast from which the head of the working sail is set.

(c) A headsail may be sheeted or attached at its clew to a spinnaker pole or whisker pole, provided that a spinnaker is not set.

50.4 Headsails
The difference between a headsail and a spinnaker is that the mid-girth of a headsail, measured from the mid-points of its luff and leech, does not exceed 50% of the length of its foot, and no other intermediate girth exceeds a percentage similarly proportional to its distance from the head of the sail. A sail tacked down behind the foremost mast is not a headsail.

51 MOVABLE BALLAST
All movable ballast shall be properly stowed, and water, dead weight or ballast shall not be moved for the purpose of changing trim or stability. Floorboards, bulkheads, doors, stairs and water tanks shall be left in place and all cabin fixtures kept on board.

52 MANUAL POWER
A boat's standing rigging, running rigging, spars and movable hull appendages shall be adjusted and operated only by manual power.

53 SKIN FRICTION
A boat shall not eject or release a substance, such as a polymer, or have specially textured surfaces that could improve the character of the flow of water inside the boundary layer.

54 FORESTAYS AND HEADSAIL TACKS
Forestays and headsail tacks, except those of spinnaker staysails when the boat is not close-hauled, shall be attached approximately on a boat's centreline.

PART 5 – PROTESTS, REDRESS, HEARINGS, MISCONDUCT AND APPEALS

Section A – Protests; Redress; Rule 69 Action

60 RIGHT TO PROTEST; RIGHT TO REQUEST REDRESS OR RULE 69 ACTION

60.1   A boat may

(a) protest another boat, but not for an alleged breach of a rule of Part 2 unless she was involved in or saw the incident; or

(b) request redress.

60.2   A race committee may

(a) protest a boat, but not as a result of a report from an *interested party* or information in an invalid *protest* or in a request for redress;

(b) request redress for a boat; or

(c) report to the protest committee requesting action under rule 69.1(a).

60.3   A protest committee may

(a) protest a boat, but not as a result of a report from an *interested party* or information in an invalid *protest* or in a request for redress. However, it may protest a boat

(1) if it learns of an incident involving her that may have resulted in injury or serious damage, or

(2) if during the hearing of a valid *protest* it learns that the boat, although not a *party* to the hearing, was involved in the incident and may have broken a *rule*;

(b) call a hearing to consider redress; or

(c) act under rule 69.1(a).

61   PROTEST REQUIREMENTS

61.1   Informing the Protestee

(a)   A boat intending to protest shall inform the other boat at the first reasonable opportunity. When her *protest* concerns an incident in the racing area that she is involved in or sees, she shall hail 'Protest' and conspicuously display a red flag at the first reasonable opportunity for each. She shall display the flag until she is no longer *racing*. However,

(1)   if the other boat is beyond hailing distance, the protesting boat need not hail but she shall inform the other boat at the first reasonable opportunity;

(2)   if the hull length of the protesting boat is less than 6 metres, she need not display a red flag;

(3)   if the incident results in damage or injury that is obvious to the boats involved and one of them intends to protest, the requirements of this rule do not apply to her, but she shall attempt to inform the other boat within the time limit of rule 61.3.

(b)   A race committee or protest committee intending to protest a boat shall inform her as soon as reasonably possible. However, if the *protest* arises from an incident the committee observes in the racing area, it shall inform the boat after the race within the time limit of rule 61.3.

(c)   If the protest committee decides to protest a boat under rule 60.3(a)(2), it shall inform her as soon as reasonably possible, close the current hearing, proceed as required by rules 61.2 and 63, and hear the original and the new *protests* together.

61.2   Protest Contents

A *protest* shall be in writing and identify

(a)   the protestor and protestee;
(b)   the incident, including where and when it occurred;
(c)   any *rule* the protestor believes was broken; and
(d)   the name of the protestor's representative.

However, if requirement (b) is met, requirement (a) may be met at any time before the hearing, and requirements (c) and (d) may be met before or during the hearing.

61.3   Protest Time Limit

A *protest* by a boat, or by the race committee or protest committee about an incident the committee observes in the racing area, shall be delivered to the race office no later than the time limit stated in the sailing instructions. If none is stated, the time limit is two hours after the last boat in the race *finishes*. Other race committee or protest committee *protests* shall be delivered to the race office within two hours after the committee receives the relevant information. The protest committee shall extend the time if there is good reason to do so.

62   REDRESS

**62.1   **A request for redress or a protest committee's decision to consider redress shall be based on a claim or possibility that a boat's score in a race or series has, through no fault of her own, been made significantly worse by

(a)   an improper action or omission of the race committee, protest committee or organizing authority;

(b)   injury or physical damage because of the action of a boat that was breaking a rule of Part 2 or of a vessel not *racing* that was required to keep clear;

(c)   giving help (except to herself or her crew) in compliance with rule 1.1; or

(d)   a boat against which a penalty has been imposed under rule 2 or disciplinary action has been taken under rule 69.1(b).

**62.2   **The request shall be made in writing within the time limit of rule 61.3 or within two hours of the relevant incident, whichever is later. The protest committee shall extend the time if there is good reason to do so. No red flag is required.

Section B – Hearings and Decisions

63   HEARINGS

63.1   Requirement for a Hearing

A boat or competitor shall not be penalized without a protest hearing, except as provided in rules 30.2, 30.3, 67, 69, A5 and P2. A decision on redress shall not be made without a hearing.

The protest committee shall hear all *protests* and requests for redress that have been delivered to the race office unless it allows a *protest* or request to be withdrawn.

63.2   Time and Place of the Hearing; Time for Parties to Prepare

All *parties* to the hearing shall be notified of the time and place of the hearing, the *protest* or redress information shall be made available to them, and they shall be allowed reasonable time to prepare for the hearing.

63.3   Right to Be Present

(a)   The *parties* to the hearing, or a representative of each, have the right to be present throughout the hearing of all the evidence. When a *protest* claims a breach of a rule of Part 2, 3 or 4, the representatives of boats shall have been on board at the time of the incident, unless there is good reason for the protest committee to rule otherwise. Any witness, other than a member of the protest committee, shall be excluded except when giving evidence.

(b)   If a *party* to the hearing does not come to the hearing, the protest committee may nevertheless decide the protest or request for redress. If the *party* was unavoidably absent, the committee may reopen the hearing.

63.4   Interested Party

A member of a protest committee who is an *interested party* shall not take any further part in the hearing but may appear as a witness. A *party* to the hearing who believes a member of the protest committee is an *interested party* shall object as soon as possible.

63.5   Validity of the Protest or Request for Redress

At the beginning of the hearing the protest committee shall decide whether all requirements for the *protest* or request for redress have been met, after first taking any evidence it considers necessary. If all requirements have been met, the *protest* or request is valid and the hearing shall be continued. If not, it shall be closed. If the *protest* has been made under rule 60.3(a)(1), the protest committee shall also determine whether or not injury or serious damage resulted from the incident in question. If not, the hearing shall be closed.

63.6 Taking Evidence and Finding Facts

The protest committee shall take the evidence of the *parties* to the hearing and of their witnesses and other evidence it considers necessary. A member of the protest committee who saw the incident may give evidence. A *party* to the hearing may question any person who gives evidence. The committee shall then find the facts and base its decision on them.

63.7 Conflict between Rules

If there is a conflict between a *rule* in the notice of race and one in the sailing instructions that must be resolved before the protest committee can decide a *protest* or request for redress, the committee shall apply the *rule* that it believes will provide the fairest result for all boats affected.

63.8 Protests between Boats in Different Races

A *protest* between boats sailing in different races conducted by different organizing authorities shall be heard by a protest committee acceptable to those authorities.

64 DECISIONS

64.1 Penalties and Exoneration

(a) When the protest committee decides that a boat that is a *party* to a protest hearing has broken a *rule*, it shall disqualify her unless some other penalty applies. A penalty shall be imposed whether or not the applicable *rule* was mentioned in the *protest*.

(b) When as a consequence of breaking a *rule* a boat has compelled another boat to break a *rule*, rule 64.1(a) does not apply to the other boat and she shall be exonerated.

(c) If a boat has broken a *rule* when not *racing*, her penalty shall apply to the race sailed nearest in time to that of the incident.

64.2 Decisions on Redress

When the protest committee decides that a boat is entitled to redress under rule 62, it shall make as fair an arrangement as possible for all boats affected, whether or not they asked for redress. This may be to adjust the scoring (see rule A10 for some examples) or finishing times of boats, to *abandon* the race, to let the results stand or to make some other arrangement. When in doubt about the facts or probable results of any arrangement for the race or series, especially before *abandoning* the race, the protest committee shall take evidence from appropriate sources.

64.3   Decisions on Measurement Protests

(a) When the protest committee finds that deviations in excess of tolerances specified in the class rules were caused by damage or normal wear and do not improve the performance of the boat, it shall not penalize her. However, the boat shall not *race* again until the deviations have been corrected, except when the protest committee decides there is or has been no reasonable opportunity to do so.

(b) When the protest committee is in doubt about the meaning of a measurement rule, it shall refer its questions, together with the relevant facts, to an authority responsible for interpreting the rule. In making its decision, the committee shall be bound by the reply of the authority.

(c) When a boat disqualified under a measurement rule states in writing that she intends to appeal, she may compete in subsequent races without changes to the boat, but shall be disqualified if she fails to appeal or the appeal is decided against her.

(d) Measurement costs arising from a *protest* involving a measurement rule shall be paid by the unsuccessful *party* unless the protest committee decides otherwise.

65   INFORMING THE PARTIES AND OTHERS

65.1 After making its decision, the protest committee shall promptly inform the *parties* to the hearing of the facts found, the applicable *rules*, the decision, the reasons for it, and any penalties imposed or redress given.

65.2 A *party* to the hearing is entitled to receive the above information in writing, provided she asks for it in writing from the protest committee within seven days of being informed of the decision. The committee shall then promptly provide the information, including, when relevant, a diagram of the incident prepared or endorsed by the committee.

65.3 When the protest committee penalizes a boat under a measurement rule, it shall send the above information to the relevant measurement authorities.

66   REOPENING A HEARING

The protest committee may reopen a hearing when it decides that it may have made a significant error, or when significant new evidence becomes available within a reasonable time. It shall reopen a hearing when required by the national authority under rule F5. A *party* to the hearing may ask for a reopening no later than 24 hours after being informed of the decision. When a hearing is reopened, a majority of the members of the protest committee shall, if possible, be members of the original protest committee.

67   RULE 42 AND HEARING REQUIREMENT

When so stated in the sailing instructions, the protest committee may penalize without a hearing a boat that has broken rule 42, provided that a member of the committee or its designated observer has seen the incident, and a disqualification under this rule shall not be excluded from the boat's series score. A boat so penalized shall be informed by notification in the race results.

68   DAMAGES

The question of damages arising from a breach of any *rule* shall be governed by the prescriptions, if any, of the national authority.

Section C – Gross Misconduct

69   ALLEGATIONS OF GROSS MISCONDUCT

69.1   Action by a Protest Committee

(a) When a protest committee, from its own observation or a report received from any source, believes that a competitor may have committed a gross breach of a *rule*, good manners or sportsmanship, or may have brought the sport into disrepute, it may call a hearing. The protest committee shall promptly inform the competitor in writing of the alleged misconduct and of the time and place of the hearing.

(b) A protest committee of at least three members shall conduct the hearing, following rules 63.2, 63.3, 63.4 and 63.6. If it decides that the competitor committed the alleged misconduct it shall either

    (1) warn the competitor or

    (2) impose a penalty by excluding the competitor and, when appropriate, disqualifying a boat, from a race or the remaining races or all races of the series, or by

taking other action within its jurisdiction. A disqualification under this rule shall not be excluded from
the boat's series score.

(c)   The protest committee shall promptly report a penalty, but
not a warning, to the national authorities of the venue, of
the competitor and of the boat owner.

(d)   If there is good reason for the competitor not to attend the
hearing, the protest committee shall postpone it. However,
if the competitor has left the event and as a result cannot
reasonably be expected to attend a hearing, the protest
committee shall not conduct one. Instead, it shall collect
all available information and, if the allegation seems justi-
fied, make a report to the relevant national authorities.

(e)   When the protest committee has left the event and a
report alleging misconduct is received, the race committee
or organizing authority may appoint a new protest committee to proceed under this rule.

69.2   Action by a National Authority

(a)   When a national authority receives a report required by rule
69.1(c) or 69.1(d), a report alleging a gross breach of a *rule*,
good manners or sportsmanship, or a report alleging conduct
that has brought the sport into disrepute, it may conduct an
investigation and, when appropriate, shall conduct a hearing.
It may then take any disciplinary action within its jurisdiction it considers appropriate against the competitor or
boat, or other person involved, including suspending eligibility, permanently or for a specified period of time, to
compete in any event held within its jurisdiction, and suspending ISAF eligibility under ISAF Regulation 19.

(b)   The national authority of a competitor shall also suspend
the ISAF eligibility of the competitor as required in ISAF
Regulation 19.

(c)   The national authority shall promptly report a suspension
of eligibility under rule 69.2(a) to the ISAF, and to the
national authorities of the person or the owner of the
boat suspended if they are not members of the suspending
national authority.

69.3   Action by the ISAF

Upon receipt of a report required by rule 69.2(c) or ISAF
Regulation 19, the ISAF shall inform all national authorities,
which may also suspend eligibility for events held within their

jurisdiction. The ISAF Executive Committee shall suspend the competitor's ISAF eligibility as required in ISAF Regulation 19 if the competitor's national authority does not do so.

Section D – Appeals

70 APPEALS; CONFIRMATION OR CORRECTION OF DECISIONS; RULE INTERPRETATIONS

70.1 Provided that the right of appeal has not been denied under rule 70.4, a *party* to a hearing may appeal a protest committee's decision or its procedures, but not the facts found, to the national authority of the venue.

70.2 A protest committee may request confirmation or correction of its decision.

70.3 A club or other organization affiliated to a national authority may request an interpretation of the *rules*, provided that no *protest* or request for redress that may be appealed is involved. The interpretation shall not be used for changing a previous protest committee decision.

70.4 There shall be no appeal from the decisions of an international jury constituted in compliance with Appendix N. Furthermore, if the notice of race and the sailing instructions so state, the right of appeal may be denied provided that

(a) it is essential to determine promptly the result of a race that will qualify a boat to compete in a later stage of an event or a subsequent event (a national authority may prescribe that its approval is required for such a procedure);

(b) a national authority so approves for a particular event open only to entrants under its own jurisdiction; or

(c) a national authority after consultation with the ISAF so approves for a particular event, provided the protest committee is constituted as required by Appendix N, except that only two members of the protest committee need be International Judges.

70.5 Appeals and requests shall conform to Appendix F.

71   **APPEAL DECISIONS**

71.1   No *interested party* or member of the protest committee shall take any part in the discussion or decision on an appeal or a request for confirmation or correction.

71.2   The national authority may uphold, change or reverse the protest committee's decision; declare the *protest* or request for redress invalid; or return the *protest* or request for the hearing to be reopened, or for a new hearing and decision by the same or a different protest committee.

71.3   When from the facts found by the protest committee the national authority decides that a boat that was a *party* to a protest hearing broke a *rule*, it shall penalize her, whether or not that boat or that *rule* was mentioned in the protest committee's decision.

71.4   The decision of the national authority shall be final. The national authority shall send its decision in writing to all *parties* to the hearing and the protest committee, who shall be bound by the decision.

PART 6 – ENTRY & QUALIFICATION

75   **ENTERING A RACE**

75.1   To enter a race, a boat shall comply with the requirements of the organizing authority of the race. She shall be entered by

(a)   a member of a club or other organization affiliated to an ISAF member national authority,

(b)   such a club or organization, or

(c)   a member of an ISAF member national authority.

75.2   Competitors shall comply with ISAF Regulation 19, Eligibility Code.

76   **EXCLUSION OF BOATS OR COMPETITORS**

76.1   The organizing authority or the race committee may reject or cancel the entry of a boat or exclude a competitor, subject to rule 76.2, provided it does so before the start of the first race and states the reason for doing so. However, the organizing authority or the race committee shall not reject or cancel the entry of a boat or exclude a competitor because of advertising, provided the boat or competitor complies with ISAF Regulation 20, Advertising Code.

76.2   At world and continental championships no entry within stated quotas shall be rejected or cancelled without first obtaining the approval of the relevant international class association (or the Offshore Racing Council) or the ISAF.

77   **IDENTIFICATION ON SAILS**
A boat shall comply with the requirements of Appendix G governing class insignia, national letters and numbers on sails.

78   **COMPLIANCE WITH CLASS RULES; CERTIFICATES**

78.1   A boat's owner and any other person in charge shall ensure that the boat is maintained to comply with her class rules and that her measurement or rating certificate, if any, remains valid.

78.2   When a *rule* requires a certificate to be produced before a boat *races*, and it is not produced, the boat may *race* provided that the race committee receives a statement signed by the person in charge that a valid certificate exists and that it will be given to the race committee before the end of the event. If the certificate is not received in time, the boat shall be disqualified from all races of the event.

78.3   When a measurer for an event decides that a boat or personal equipment does not comply with the class rules, he shall report the matter in writing to the race committee, which shall protest the boat.

79   **ADVERTISING**
A boat and her crew shall comply with ISAF Regulation 20, Advertising Code.

80   **RESCHEDULED RACES**
When a race has been rescheduled, rule 36 applies and all boats entered in the original race shall be notified and, unless disqualified under rule 30.3, be entitled to sail the rescheduled race. New entries that meet the entry requirements of the original race may be accepted at the discretion of the race committee.

PART 7 – RACE ORGANIZATION

85 GOVERNING RULES

The organizing authority, race committee and protest committee shall be governed by the *rules* in the conduct and judging of races.

86 CHANGES TO THE RACING RULES

86.1 A racing rule shall not be changed unless permitted in the rule itself or as follows:

(a) Prescriptions of a national authority may change a racing rule, but not the Definitions; a rule in the Introduction; Sportsmanship and the Rules; Part 1, 2 or 7; rule 42, 43.1, 43.2, 69, 70, 71, 75, 76.2 or 79; a rule of an appendix that changes one of these rules; Appendix H or N; or ISAF Regulation 19, 20 or 21.

(b) Sailing instructions may change a racing rule by referring specifically to it and stating the change, but not rule 76.1, Appendix F, or a rule listed in rule 86.1(a).

(c) Class rules may change only racing rules 42, 49, 50, 51, 52, 53 and 54.

86.2 In exception to rule 86.1, the ISAF may in limited circumstances (see ISAF Regulation 31.1.3) authorize changes to the racing rules for a specific international event. The authorization shall be stated in a letter of approval to the event organizing authority and in the notice of race and sailing instructions, and the letter shall be posted on the event's official notice board.

86.3 If a national authority so prescribes, these restrictions do not apply if rules are changed to develop or test proposed rules. The national authority may prescribe that its approval is required for such changes.

87 CHANGES TO NATIONAL AUTHORITY PRESCRIPTIONS

A national authority may restrict changes to its prescriptions with a prescription to this rule. If it does so, that prescription shall not be changed or deleted by sailing instructions.

88   ORGANIZING AUTHORITY; NOTICE OF RACE; APPOINTMENT OF RACE OFFICIALS

88.1   Organizing Authority
Races shall be organized by an organizing authority, which shall be

(a)   the ISAF;

(b)   a member national authority of the ISAF;

(c)   a club or other organization affiliated to a national authority;

(d)   a class association, either with the approval of a national authority or in conjunction with an affiliated club;

(e)   an unaffiliated body in conjunction with an affiliated club where the body is owned and controlled by the club. The national authority of the club may prescribe that its approval is required for such an event; or

(f)   if approved by the ISAF and the national authority of the club, an unaffiliated body in conjunction with an affiliated club where the body is not owned and controlled by the club.

88.2   Notice of Race; Appointment of Race Officials

(a)   The organizing authority shall publish a notice of race that conforms to rule J1. The notice of race may be changed provided adequate notice is given.

(b)   The organizing authority shall appoint a race committee and, when appropriate, appoint a protest committee and umpires. However, the race committee, an international jury and umpires may be appointed by the ISAF as provided in the ISAF regulations.

89   RACE COMMITTEE; SAILING INSTRUCTIONS; SCORING

89.1   Race Committee
The race committee shall conduct races as directed by the organizing authority and as required by the *rules*.

89.2   Sailing Instructions

(a)   The race committee shall publish written sailing instructions that conform to rule J2.

(b) The sailing instructions for an international event shall include, in English, the applicable prescriptions of the national authority.

(c) Changes to the sailing instructions shall be in writing and posted within the required time on the official notice board or, on the water, communicated to each boat before her warning signal. Oral changes may be given only on the water, and only if the procedure is stated in the sailing instructions.

89.3 Scoring

(a) The race committee shall score a race or series as provided in Appendix A using the Low Point System, unless the sailing instructions specify the Bonus Point System or some other system. A race shall be scored if it is not *abandoned* and if one boat sails the course in compliance with rule 28.1 and *finishes* within the time limit, if any, even if she retires after *finishing* or is disqualified.

(b) When a scoring system provides for excluding one or more race scores from a boat's series score, the score for disqualification under rule 2; rule 30.3's next-to-last sentence; rule 42 if rule 67, P2.2 or P2.3 applies; or rule 69.1(b)(2) shall not be excluded. The next-worse score shall be excluded instead.

90 PROTEST COMMITTEE
A protest committee shall be

(a) a committee appointed by the organizing authority or race committee, or

(b) an international jury appointed by the organizing authority or as prescribed in the ISAF regulations and meeting the requirements of Appendix N. A national authority may prescribe that its approval is required for the appointment of international juries for races within its jurisdiction, except ISAF events or when international juries are appointed by the ISAF under rule 88.2(b).

APPENDIX A – SCORING

See rule 89.3.

A1   **NUMBER OF RACES**

The number of races scheduled and the number required to be completed to constitute a series shall be stated in the sailing instructions.

A2   **SERIES SCORES**

Each boat's series score shall be the total of her race scores excluding her worst score. (The sailing instructions may make a different arrangement by providing, for example, that no score will be excluded, that two or more scores will be excluded, or that a specified number of scores will be excluded if a specified number of races are completed. A race is completed if scored; see rule 89.3(a).) If a boat has two or more equal worst scores, the score(s) for the race(s) sailed earliest in the series shall be excluded. The boat with the lowest series score wins and others shall be ranked accordingly.

A3   **STARTING TIMES AND FINISHING PLACES**

The time of a boat's starting signal shall be her starting time, and the order in which boats *finish* a race shall determine their finishing places. However, when a handicap or rating system is used a boat's corrected time shall determine her finishing place.

A4   **LOW POINT AND BONUS POINT SYSTEMS**

Most series are scored using either the Low Point System or the Bonus Point System. The Low Point System uses a boat's finishing place as her race score. The Bonus Point System benefits the first six finishers because of the greater difficulty in advancing from fourth place to third, for example, than from fourteenth place to thirteenth. The Low Point System will apply unless the sailing instructions specify another system; see rule 89.3(a). If the Bonus Point System is chosen it can be made to apply by stating in the sailing instructions that 'The Bonus Point System of Appendix A will apply.'

A4.1   Each boat *starting* and *finishing* and not thereafter retiring, being penalized or given redress shall be scored points as follows:

Finishing place	Low Point System	Bonus Point System
First	1	0
Second	2	3
Third	3	5.7
Fourth	4	8
Fifth	5	10
Sixth	6	11.7
Seventh	7	13
Each place thereafter	Add 1 point	Add 1 point

A4.2   A boat that did not *start*, did not *finish*, retired after *finishing* or was disqualified shall be scored points for the finishing place one more than the number of boats entered in the series. A boat penalized under rule 30.2 or 44.3 shall be scored points as provided in rule 44.3(c).

A5   SCORES DETERMINED BY THE RACE COMMITTEE
A boat that did not *start*, comply with rule 30.2 or 30.3, or *finish*, or that takes a penalty under rule 44.3 or retires after *finishing*, shall be scored accordingly by the race committee without a hearing. Only the protest committee may take other scoring actions that worsen a boat's score.

A6   CHANGES IN PLACES AND SCORES OF OTHER BOATS

A6.1   If a boat is disqualified from a race or retires after *finishing*, each boat with a worse finishing place shall be moved up one place.

A6.2   If the protest committee decides to give redress by adjusting a boat's score, the scores of other boats shall not be changed unless the protest committee decides otherwise.

A7   RACE TIES
If boats are tied at the finishing line or if a handicap or rating system is used and boats have equal corrected times, the points for the place for which the boats have tied and for the place(s) immediately below shall be added together and divided equally. Boats tied for a race prize shall share it or be given equal prizes.

A8   **SERIES TIES**

A8.1   If there is a series score tie between two or more boats, each boat's race scores shall be listed in order of best to worst, and at the first point(s) where there is a difference the tie shall be broken in favour of the boat(s) with the best score(s). No excluded scores shall be used.

A8.2   If a tie remains between two or more boats, they shall be ranked in order of their scores in the last race. Any remaining ties shall be broken by using the tied boats' scores in the next-to-last race and so on until all ties are broken. These scores shall be used even if some of them are excluded scores.

A9   **RACE SCORES IN A SERIES LONGER THAN A REGATTA**
For a series that is held over a period of time longer than a regatta, a boat that came to the starting area but did not *start*, did not *finish*, retired after *finishing* or was disqualified shall be scored points for the finishing place one more than the number of boats that came to the starting area. A boat that did not come to the starting area shall be scored points for the finishing place one more than the number of boats entered in the series.

A10   **GUIDANCE ON REDRESS**
If the protest committee decides to give redress by adjusting a boat's score for a race, it is advised to consider scoring her

    (a) points equal to the average, to the nearest tenth of a point (0.05 to be rounded upward), of her points in all the races in the series except the race in question;

    (b) points equal to the average, to the nearest tenth of a point (0.05 to be rounded upward), of her points in all the races before the race in question; or

    (c) points based on the position of the boat in the race at the time of the incident that justified redress.

A11   **SCORING ABBREVIATIONS**
These abbreviations are recommended for recording the circumstances described:

    DNC   Did not *start*; did not come to the starting area

    DNS   Did not *start* (other than DNC and OCS)

    OCS   Did not *start*; on the course side of the starting line at her starting signal and failed to *start*, or broke rule 30.1

ZFP   20% penalty under rule 30.2
BFD   Disqualification under rule 30.3
SCP   Took a scoring penalty under rule 44.3
DNF   Did not *finish*
RAF   Retired after *finishing*
DSQ   Disqualification
DNE   Disqualification (other than DGM) not excludable under
        rule 89.3(b)
DGM   Disqualification under rule 69.1(b)(2); not excludable
RDG   Redress given

APPENDIX B – WINDSURFING COMPETITION RULES

Windsurfing competition shall be sailed under The Racing Rules of Sailing *as changed by this appendix. The term 'boat' elsewhere in the racing rules means 'board' or 'boat' as appropriate. A windsurfing event can include one or more of the following disciplines or their formats:*

Discipline	*Formats*
Racing	*Course racing; slalom; marathon*
Expression	*Wave performance; freestyle*
Speed	

In expression competition a board's performance is judged on skill and variety rather than speed and is organized using elimination series. Either wave performance or freestyle competition is organized, depending on the wave conditions at the venue. In speed competition, a 'round' consists of one or more speed runs in which the boards take turns sailing the course at intervals. In the racing discipline a marathon race is a race scheduled to last more than one hour.

In slalom racing or expression competition, 'heat' means one elimination contest, a 'round' consists of one or more heats, and an elimination series consists of a maximum of four rounds.

B1 DEFINITIONS

B1.1 The following additional definitions apply:

Beach Start When the starting line is on the beach, or so close to the beach that the competitor must stand in the water to *start*, the start is a *beach start*.

Capsized A board is *capsized* when her sail or the competitor is in the water.

B1.2 The following definitions apply only to expression competition:

Coming In and Going Out
A board sailing in the same direction as the incoming surf is *coming in*. A board sailing in the direction opposite to the incoming surf is *going out*.

Jumping A board is *jumping* when she takes off at the top of a wave while *going out*.

Overtaking A board is *overtaking* from the moment she gains an *overlap* from *clear astern* until the moment she is *clear ahead* of the *overtaken* board.

Possession The first board sailing shoreward immediately in front of a wave has *possession* of that wave. However, when it is impossible to determine which board is first the *windward* board has *possession*.

Recovering A board is *recovering* from the time her sail or, when water-starting, the competitor is out of the water until she has steerage way.

Surfing A board is *surfing* when she is on or immediately in front of a wave while *coming in*.

Transition A board changing *tacks*, or taking off while *coming in*, or one that is not *surfing*, *jumping*, *capsized* or *recovering* is in *transition*.

B2 RULES FOR ALL COMPETITION

B2.1 Changes to the Rules of Part 4

(a) Rule 42 is changed to 'A board shall be propelled only by the action of the wind on the sail, by the action of the water on the hull and by the unassisted actions of the competitor.'

(b) Add to rule 43.1(a): 'However, a competitor may wear a drinking container that shall have a capacity of at least one litre and weigh no more than 1.5 kilograms when full.'

(c) Rule 44.2 is changed so that two turns are replaced by one 360° turn with no requirement for tacks or gybes.

(d) Rules 44.3 and 44.4(a) are deleted.

(e) Add to rule 47.1: 'except as stated in rule 41.2'. (See rule B4.4.) Rule 47.2 is deleted.

B2.2 Entry and Qualification
Add to rule 78.1: 'When so prescribed by the ISAF, a numbered and dated device on a board and her centreboard, fin and rig shall serve as her measurement certificate.'

B2.3 Event Organization

(a) The last sentence of rule 89.2(c) is deleted.

(b) Add new rule 89.2(d): 'Oral instructions may be given only if the procedure is stated in the sailing instructions.'

B2.4 Identification on Sails

(a) Add to rule G1.1(a): 'The insignia shall not refer to anything other than the manufacturer or class and shall not consist of more than two letters and three numbers or an abstract design.'

(b) Rules G1.3(a), G1.3(c), G1.3(d) and G1.3(e) are changed to The class insignia shall be displayed once on each side of the sail in the area above a line projected at right angles from a point on the luff of the sail one-third of the distance from the head to the wishbone. The national letters and sail numbers shall be in the central third of that part of the sail above the wishbone, clearly separated from any advertising, and placed at different heights on the two sides of the sail, those on the starboard side being uppermost.

B3 **RULES FOR RACING COMPETITION**

B3.1 **When Boards Meet**

(a) Rule 13 becomes rule 13.1. Add new rule 13.2:
> A board gybing shall *keep clear* of other boards. During that time rules 10, 11 and 12 do not apply. If two boards are subject to this rule at the same time, the one on the other's port side or the one astern shall *keep clear*.

(b) Rules 17, 18.2(b), 18.2(c) and 18.3 are deleted.

(c) Rule 21 becomes rule 21.1. Add new rule 21.2: 'A *capsized* board shall not take an action that hinders another board.'

(d) Add new rule 22.3: 'A board shall not sail in the course area defined in the sailing instructions when races are taking place except in her own race.'

(e) Add new rule 23:

23 **SAIL OUT OF THE WATER WHEN STARTING**
When approaching the starting line to *start*, a board shall have her sail out of the water and in a normal position, except when accidentally *capsized*.

B3.2 **Starting Races**
Sailing instructions shall specify one of these starting systems.

(a) SYSTEM 1   See rule 26, Starting Races.

(b) SYSTEM 2   Races shall be started by using the following signals. Times shall be taken from the visual signals; the absence of a sound signal shall be disregarded.

Signal	Flag and sound	Minutes before starting signal
Attention	Class flag or heat number	5
	Attention signal removed	4
Warning	Red flag; 1 sound	3
	Red flag removed	2
Preparatory	Yellow flag; 1 sound	1
	Yellow flag removed	1/2
Starting	Green flag; 1 sound	0

(c) SYSTEM 3 (FOR BEACH STARTS)
    (1) Before her start each board in a heat or class shall draw a number for her station on the starting line. The stations shall be numbered so that station 1 is the most windward one.
    (2) After boards have been called to take their positions, the race committee shall make the preparatory signal by displaying a red flag with one sound. The starting signal shall be made, at any time after the preparatory signal, by removing the red flag with one sound.
    (3) After the starting signal each board shall take the shortest route from her starting station to her windsurfing position in the water (with both of the competitor's feet on the board).

B3.3 Other Rules for the Conduct of a Race
(a) Add new rule 29.3:

    29.3 Recall for a Slalom Race
    (a) When at a board's starting signal for a slalom race or heat any part of her hull, crew or equipment is on the course side of the starting line, the race committee shall signal a general recall.
    (b) If the race committee acts under rule 29.3(a) and the board is identified, she shall be disqualified without a hearing, even if the race or heat is *postponed* or *abandoned*. The race committee shall hail or display her sail number, and she shall leave the course area immediately. If the race or heat is restarted or resailed, she shall not sail in it.

(b) Change rule 31 to 'A board may touch a *mark* but shall not hold on to it.'

B4 RULES FOR EXPRESSION COMPETITION

B4.1 Right-of-Way Rules
These rules replace all rules of Part 2.

(a) COMING IN AND GOING OUT
    A board *coming in* shall *keep clear* of a board *going out*. When two boards are *going out* or *coming in* while on the same wave, or when neither is *going out* or *coming in*, the board on *port tack* shall *keep clear* of the one on *starboard tack*.

(b)   BOARDS ON THE SAME WAVE, COMING IN
When two or more boards are on a wave *coming in*, a board that does not have *possession* shall *keep clear*.

(c)   CLEAR ASTERN, CLEAR AHEAD AND OVERTAKING
A board *clear astern* and not on a wave shall *keep clear* of a board *clear ahead*. An overtaking board that is not on a wave shall *keep clear*.

(d)   TRANSITION
A board in *transition* shall *keep clear* of one that is not. When two boards are in *transition* at the same time, the one on the other's port side or the one astern shall *keep clear*.

B4.2   **Starting and Ending Heats**
Heats shall be started and ended by using the following signals:

(a)   STARTING A HEAT
Each flag shall be removed when the next flag is displayed.

Signal	Flag and sound	Minutes before starting signal
Attention	Heat number	3
Warning	Red flag; 1 sound	2
Preparatory	Yellow flag; 1 sound	1
Starting	Green flag; 1 sound	0

(b)   ENDING A HEAT

Signal	Flag and sound	Minutes before ending signal
End warning	Green flag removed; 1 sound	1
Ending	Red flag; 1 sound	0

B4.3   **Registration of Sails; Course Area; Heat Duration**

(a)   Boards shall register with the race committee the colours and other particulars of their sails, or their identification according to another method stated in the sailing instructions, no later than the starting signal for the heat two heats before their own.

(b) The course area shall be defined in the sailing instructions and posted on the official notice board not later than 30 minutes before the starting signal for the first heat. A board shall be scored only while sailing in the course area.

(c) Any change in heat duration shall be announced by the race committee not later than fifteen minutes before the starting signal for the first heat in the next round.

B4.4   Outside Help

Rule 41 becomes rule 41.1. Add new rule 41.2:

An assistant may provide replacement equipment to a board but shall keep clear of other boards competing. A board whose assistant fails to keep clear shall be penalized. The penalty shall be at the discretion of the protest committee.

B5   ELIMINATION SERIES FOR SLALOM RACING AND EXPRESSION COMPETITION

Rules B5.1–B5.5 apply to slalom racing or expression competition organized by using elimination series in which boards compete in heats.

B5.1   Elimination Series Procedure

(a) Competition shall take the form of one or more elimination series. Each of them shall consist of either a maximum of four rounds in a single elimination series where only a number of the best scorers advance, or a maximum of ten rounds in a double elimination series where boards have more than one opportunity to advance.

(b) Boards shall sail one against another in pairs, or in groups determined by the elimination ladder. The selected form of competition shall not be changed while a round remains uncompleted.

B5.2   Seeding and Ranking Lists

(a) When a seeding or ranking list is used to establish the heats of the first round, places 1–8 (four heats) or 1–16 (eight heats) shall be distributed evenly among the heats.

(b) For a subsequent elimination series, if any, boards shall be reassigned to new heats according to a seeding list based on the current overall standings.

(c) The organizing authority's seeding decisions are final and are not grounds for a request for redress.

B5.3 **Heat Schedule**
The schedule of heats shall be posted on the official notice board not later than 30 minutes before the starting signal for the first heat.

B5.4 **Advancement and Byes**
(a) In slalom racing and freestyle competition, the boards in each heat to advance to the next round shall be announced by the race committee not later than 30 minutes before the starting signal for the first heat. The number advancing may be changed by the protest committee as a result of a redress decision.

(b) In expression competition, any first-round byes shall be assigned to the highest-seeded boards.

(c) In wave performance competition, only the winner of each heat shall advance to the next round.

(d) In freestyle competition, boards shall advance to the next round as follows: from an eight-board heat, the best four advance, and the winner will sail against the fourth and the second against the third; from a four-board heat, the best two advance and will sail against each other.

B5.5 **Finals**
(a) The final shall consist of a maximum of three races. The race committee shall announce the number of races to be sailed in the final not later than five minutes before the warning signal for the first final race.

(b) A runners-up final may be sailed after the final. All boards in the semifinal heats that failed to qualify for the final may compete in it.

B6 **RULES FOR SPEED COMPETITION**

B6.1 **General Rules**
All rules of Part 2 are replaced by relevant parts of this rule.

(a) BEACH AND WATER STARTING
     A board shall not *beach start* or water start on the course
     or in the starting area, except to sail off the course to avoid
     boards that are *starting* or *racing*.

(b) LEAVING THE COURSE AREA
     A board leaving the course area shall *keep clear* of boards
     racing.

(c) COURSE CONTROL
     When the race committee points an orange flag at a
     board, she shall immediately leave the course area.

(d) RETURNING TO THE STARTING AREA
     A board returning to the starting area shall keep clear of
     the course.

(e) RUN; ROUND
     The maximum number of runs to be made by each board
     in a round shall be announced by the race committee not
     later than 30 minutes before the starting signal for the
     first round.

(f) DURATION OF A ROUND
     The duration of a round shall be announced by the race
     committee not later than 30 minutes before the starting
     signal for the next round.

(g) CONDITIONS FOR ESTABLISHING A RECORD
     The minimum distance for a world record is 500 metres.
     Other records may be established over shorter distances.
     The course shall be defined by posts and transits ashore or
     by buoys afloat. Transits shall not converge.

B6.2 **Starting System for Speed Competition**
Rounds shall be started and ended by using the following
signals. Each flag shall be removed when the next flag is
displayed.

(a) STARTING A ROUND

Signal	*Flag*	*Meaning*
Stand-by	Red flag	Course closed
Course closed	AP and red flag	Course closed; will open shortly
Preparatory	Yellow flag	Course will open in 5 minutes
Starting	Green flag	Course is open

(b) ENDING A ROUND

Signal	Flag	Meaning
End warning	Green and yellow flag	Course will be closed in 5 minutes
Extension	Green flag and L	Current round extended by 15 minutes
Round ended	Red flag and L	A new round will be started shortly

B6.3 Penalties

(a) If a board fails to comply with a warning by the race committee, she may be cautioned and her sail number shall be posted on a notice board near the finishing line.

(b) If a board is cautioned a second time during the same round, she shall be suspended by the race committee from the remainder of the round and her sail number shall be posted on the official notice board.

(c) A board observed in the course area while suspended shall be disqualified from the competition without a hearing and none of her previous times or results shall be valid.

(d) Any breach of the verification rules may result in a suspension from the competition for any period.

B6.4 Verification

(a) An observer appointed by the World Sailing Speed Record Council (WSSRC) shall be present and verify run times and speeds at world record attempts. The race committee shall verify run times and speeds at other record attempts.

(b) A competitor shall not enter the timing control area or discuss any timing matter directly with the timing organization. Any timing question shall be directed to the race committee.

B7   PROTESTS, REDRESS, HEARINGS AND APPEALS

B7.1 (a) Add after the third sentence of rule 61.1(a): 'She shall inform the race committee of her intention to protest immediately after she *finishes* or retires.'

(b) Rule 61.2 is retitled rule 61.2(a), Course and Marathon Racing. Add new rule 61.2(b):
SLALOM RACING AND OTHER DISCIPLINES
A *protest* shall be made orally immediately following the heat in which the incident occurred.

B7.2 Add new rule 62.1(e): 'a board that failed to *keep clear* and retired or was penalized.'

B7.3 In rule 62.2, after 'writing' add: 'except in an elimination series'.

B7.4 Rule 63.2 becomes rule 63.2(a). Add new rule 63.2(b): 'In an elimination series, the protest committee may hear a *protest* on the beach or water immediately after the heat.'

B7.5 Begin rule 65.2 with the addition 'Except in an elimination series'.

B7.6 Rule 67 is deleted.

B7.7 Add new rule 70.6: 'Appeals are not permitted in slalom racing and expression competition.'

B8 **SCORING**

B8.1 **Overall Scores**
If an event includes more than one discipline or format the sailing instructions shall state how the overall score is to be calculated.

B8.2 **Series Scores**
Rule A2 is changed to:
Each board's series score shall be the total of her race, elimination series or speed round scores with the number of her worst scores excluded as follows:

Course races, speed rounds	Slalom and expression elimination series	Number excluded
1–3	1–2	0
4–6	3–4	1
7–10	5–7	2
11–15	8 or more	3
16 or more		4

If a board has two or more equal worst scores, the score(s) for the race(s) sailed earliest in the series shall be excluded. The board with the lowest series score wins and others shall be ranked accordingly. Rules B8.5, B8.6 and B8.7 contain exceptions to this rule.

B8.3   **Scoring Systems**

(a)   Rule A4 is retitled 'Low Point and Alternative Systems' and its preamble is deleted. Rule A4.1 is changed to:
Each board starting and finishing and not thereafter retiring, being penalized or given redress shall be scored points as follows:

Finishing place	Low Point System	Alternative System
First	1	0.7
Second	2	2
Third	3	3
Each place thereafter	Add 1 point	Add 1 point

(b)   Add to the end of the first sentence of rule A4.2: 'or, in an elimination series, the number of boards in that heat'.

B8.4   **Uncompleted Heat**
When a heat cannot be completed, the points for the unscored places shall be added together and divided by the number of places in that heat. The resulting number of points, to the nearest tenth of a point (0.05 to be rounded upward), shall be given to each board entered in the heat.

B8.5   **Scoring a Final Series in Slalom**

(a)   If three final races are completed, a board's series score in the final shall be the total of her race scores excluding her worst score. Otherwise her series score shall be the total of her race scores.

(b)   A board that did not *start*, did not *finish*, retired after *finishing* or was disqualified from a final race shall be scored points equal to the total number of boards entered in the final.

B8.6   **Expression Competition Scoring**

(a)   Expression competition shall be scored by a panel of three judges. However, the panel may have a greater odd number of members, and there may be two such panels. Each judge shall give points for each manoeuvre based on the scale stated in the sailing instructions.

(b) The criteria of scoring shall be decided by the race committee and announced on the official notice board not later than 30 minutes before the starting signal for the first heat.

(c) A board's heat standing shall be determined by adding together the points given by each judge. The board with the highest score wins and other boards shall be ranked accordingly.

(d) Both semifinal heats shall have been sailed for an elimination series to be valid.

(e) Except for members of the race committee responsible for scoring the event, only competitors in the heat shall be allowed to see judges' score sheets for the heat. Each score sheet shall bear the full name of the judge.

(f) Scoring decisions of the judges shall not be grounds for a request for redress by a board.

B8.7   Speed Competition

The speeds of a board's fastest two runs in a round shall be averaged to determine her standing in that round. The board with the highest average wins and others shall be ranked accordingly.

B8.8   Series Ties

(a) RACING AND SPEED COMPETITION

Rule A8 is changed as follows for racing and speed competition:

(1) Add new rule A8.1: 'If there is a series score tie between two or more boards, it shall be broken in favour of the board(s) with the best single excluded race score(s).'

(2) Rule A8.1 becomes rule A8.2. Its beginning 'If there is a series score tie' is changed to 'If a tie remains' and its last sentence is changed to 'These scores shall be used even if some of them are excluded scores.'

(3) Rule A8.2 becomes rule A8.3 and its beginning 'If a tie remains' is changed to 'If a tie still remains'.

(b) EXPRESSION COMPETITION

Rule A8 is changed as follows for expression competition:

(1) In a heat, if there is a tie in the total points given by one or more judges, it shall be broken in favour of the

board with the higher single score in the priority category. If the categories are weighted equally, in wave performance competition the tie shall be broken in favour of the board with the higher single score in wave riding, and in freestyle competition in favour of the board with the higher score for overall impression. If a tie remains, in wave performance competition it shall be broken in favour of the board with the higher single score in the category without priority, and in freestyle competition it shall stand as the final result.

(2) If there is a tie in the series score, it shall be broken in favour of the board that scored better more times than the other board. All scores shall be used even if some of them are excluded scores.

(3) If a tie still remains, the heat shall be resailed. If this is not possible, the tie shall stand as the final result.

APPENDIX C – MATCH RACING RULES

Match races shall be sailed under The Racing Rules of Sailing *as changed by this appendix. Matches shall be umpired unless the notice of race and sailing instructions state otherwise.*

C1   TERMINOLOGY
'Competitor' means the skipper, team or boat as appropriate for the event. 'Flight' means two or more matches started in the same starting sequence.

C2   CHANGES TO THE DEFINITIONS AND THE RULES OF PARTS 2 AND 4

C2.1   The definition *Finish* is changed to:
A boat *finishes* when any part of her hull, or crew or equipment in normal position, crosses the finishing line in the direction of the course from the last *mark* after completing any penalties. However, when penalties are cancelled under rule C7.2(d) after one or both boats have *finished* each shall be recorded as *finished* when she crossed the line.

C2.2   Add to the definition *Proper Course*: 'A boat taking a penalty or manoeuvring to take a penalty is not sailing a *proper course*.'

C2.3   The last sentence of the definition *Clear Ahead* and *Clear Astern*; *Overlap* is changed to 'These terms do not apply to boats on opposite tacks unless either rule 18 applies or both boats are subject to rule 13.2.'

C2.4   Rule 13 is changed to:

13   WHILE TACKING OR GYBING

13.1   After a boat passes head to wind, she shall *keep clear* of other boats until she is on a close-hauled course.

13.2   After the foot of the mainsail of a boat sailing downwind crosses the centreline she shall *keep clear* of other boats until her mainsail has filled.

13.3   While rule 13.1 or 13.2 applies, rules 10, 11 and 12 do not. However, if two boats are subject to rule 13.1 or 13.2 at the same time, the one on the other's port side or the one astern shall *keep clear*.

C2.5   Rules 16.2 and 17.2 are deleted.

C2.6   Rule 18.3 is changed to:

If two boats were on opposite *tacks* and one of them completes a tack within the *two-length zone* to pass a rounding *mark*, and if thereafter the other boat cannot by luffing avoid becoming *overlapped* inside her, the boat that tacked shall *keep clear* and rules 15 and 18.2 do not apply. If the other boat can by luffing avoid becoming *overlapped* inside her then rule 18.2(c) shall apply as if the boats were *clear ahead* and *clear astern* at the *two-length zone*.

C2.7   When rule 19.1 applies, the following arm signals by the helmsman are required in addition to the hails:

(a)   for 'Room to tack', repeatedly and clearly pointing to windward; and

(b)   for 'You tack', repeatedly and clearly pointing at the other boat and waving the arm to windward.

C2.8   Rule 20.2 is changed to 'A boat taking a penalty shall *keep clear* of one that is not.'

C2.9   Rule 22.1 is changed to 'If reasonably possible, a boat not *racing* shall not interfere with a boat that is *racing* or an umpire boat.'

C2.10 Rule 22.2 is changed to 'Except when sailing a *proper course*, a boat shall not interfere with a boat taking a penalty or sailing on another leg.'

C2.11 Add new rule 22.3: 'When boats in different matches meet, any change of course by either boat shall be consistent with complying with a *rule* or trying to win her own match.'

C2.12 Add to the preamble of Part 4: 'Rule 42 shall also apply between the warning and preparatory signals.'

C2.13 Rule 42.2(d) is changed to 'sculling: repeated movement of the helm to propel the boat forward;'.

C3 **RACE SIGNALS AND CHANGES TO RELATED RULES**

C3.1 **Starting Signals**
The signals for starting a match shall be as follows. Times shall be taken from the visual signals; the failure of a sound signal shall be disregarded. If more than one match will be sailed, the starting signal for one match shall be the warning signal for the next match.

Time in minutes	Visual signal	Sound signal	Means
10	Flag F displayed	One	Attention signal
6	Flag F removed	None	
5	Numeral pennant displayed*	One	Warning signal
4	Flag P displayed	One	Preparatory signal
2	Blue or yellow flag or both displayed**	One**	End of pre-start entry time
0	Warning and preparatory signals removed	One	Starting signal

*Within a flight, numeral pennant 1 means Match 1, pennant 2 means Match 2, etc., unless the sailing instructions state otherwise.

**These signals shall be made only if one or both boats fail to comply with rule C4.2. The flag(s) shall be displayed until the umpires have signalled a penalty or for one minute, whichever is earlier.

C3.2 **Changes to Related Rules**
   (a) Rule 29.1 is changed to:
      (1) When at a boat's starting signal any part of her hull, crew or equipment is on the course side of the starting line or its extensions, the race committee shall promptly display a blue or yellow flag identifying the boat with one sound. The flag shall be displayed until the boat is completely on the pre-start side of the starting line or its extensions or until two minutes after her starting signal, whichever is earlier.
      (2) When at a boat's starting signal no part of her hull, crew or equipment is on the course side of the starting line or its extensions, and before she *starts* she sails to the course side across an extension, the race committee shall promptly display a blue or yellow flag identifying the boat. The flag shall be displayed until the boat is completely on the pre-start side of the starting line or its extensions or until two minutes after her starting signal, whichever is earlier.
   (b) In the race signal AP the last sentence is changed to 'The attention signal will be made 1 minute after removal unless at that time the race is *postponed* again or *abandoned.*'
   (c) In the race signal N the last sentence is changed to 'The attention signal will be made 1 minute after removal unless at that time the race is *abandoned* again or *postponed.*'

C3.3 **Finishing Line Signals**
   The race signal Blue flag or shape shall not be used.

C4 **REQUIREMENTS BEFORE THE START**

C4.1 At her preparatory signal, each boat shall be outside the line that is at a 90° angle to the starting line through the starting *mark* at her assigned end. In the race schedule pairing list, the boat listed on the left-hand side is assigned the port end and shall display a blue flag at her stern while *racing*. The other boat is assigned the starboard end and shall display a yellow flag at her stern while *racing*.

C4.2   Within the two-minute period following her preparatory signal, a boat shall cross and clear the starting line, the first time from the course side to the pre-start side.

C5   **SIGNALS BY UMPIRES**

C5.1   A green and white flag with one long sound means 'No penalty.'

C5.2   A blue or yellow flag identifying a boat with one long sound means 'The identified boat shall take a penalty by complying with rule C7.'

C5.3   A red flag with or soon after a blue or yellow flag with one long sound means 'The identified boat shall take a penalty by complying with rule C7.3(d).'

C5.4   A black flag with a blue or yellow flag and one long sound means 'The identified boat is disqualified, and the match is terminated and awarded to the other boat.'

C5.5   One short sound means 'A penalty is now completed.'

C5.6   Repetitive short sounds mean 'A boat is no longer taking a penalty and the penalty remains.'

C5.7   A blue or yellow flag or shape displayed from an umpire boat means 'The identified boat has an outstanding penalty.'

C6   **PROTESTS AND REQUESTS FOR REDRESS BY BOATS**

C6.1   A boat may protest another boat

(a)   under a rule of Part 2, except rule 14, by clearly displaying flag Y immediately after an incident in which she was involved;

(b)   under any rule not listed in rule C6.1(a) or C6.2 by clearly displaying a red flag as soon as possible after the incident.

C6.2   A boat may not protest another boat under

(a)   rule 14, unless damage or injury results;

(b)   a rule of Part 2, unless she was involved in the incident;

(c)   rule 31 or 42; or

(d)   rule C4 or C7.

C6.3   A boat intending to request redress because of circumstances that arise before she *finishes* or retires shall clearly display a red flag as soon as possible after she becomes aware of those circumstances, but not later than two minutes after *finishing* or retiring.

C6.4   (a)   A boat protesting under rule C6.1(a) shall remove flag Y before or as soon as possible after the umpires' signal.

(b)   A boat protesting under rule C6.1(b) or requesting redress under rule C6.3 shall, for her *protest* or request to be valid, keep her red flag displayed until she has so informed the umpires after *finishing* or retiring. No written *protest* or request for redress is required.

C6.5   **Umpire Decisions**

(a)   After flag Y is displayed, the umpires shall decide whether to penalize any boat. They shall signal their decision in compliance with rule C5.1, C5.2 or C5.3.

(b)   The red-flag penalty in rule C5.3 shall be used when a boat has gained control as a result of breaking a rule, but the umpires are not certain that the conditions for an additional umpire-initiated penalty have been fulfilled.

C6.6   **Protest Committee Decisions**

(a)   The protest committee may take evidence in any way it considers appropriate and may communicate its decision orally.

(b)   If the protest committee decides that a breach of a *rule* has had no significant effect on the outcome of the match, it may
    (1)   impose a penalty of one point or part of one point;
    (2)   order a resail; or
    (3)   make another arrangement it decides is equitable, which may be to impose no penalty.

(c)   The penalty for breaking rule 14 when damage or injury results will be at the discretion of the protest committee, and may include exclusion from further races in the event.

C7   **PENALTY SYSTEM**

C7.1   **Rule Changes**
Rules 31.2 and 44 are deleted.

C7.2 **All Penalties**

(a) A penalized boat may delay taking a penalty within the limitations of rule C7.3 and shall take it as follows:

(1) When on a leg of the course to a windward *mark*, she shall gybe and, as soon as reasonably possible, luff to a close-hauled course.

(2) When on a leg of the course to a leeward *mark* or the finishing line, she shall tack and, as soon as reasonably possible, bear away to a downwind course.

(b) Add to rule 2: 'When *racing*, a boat may wait for an umpire's decision before taking a penalty.'

(c) A boat completes a leg of the course when her bow crosses the extension of the line from the previous *mark* through the *mark* she is rounding, or on the last leg when she *finishes*.

(d) A penalized boat shall not be recorded as having *finished* until she takes her penalty and sails completely to the course side of the line and then *finishes*, unless the penalty is cancelled before or after she crosses the finishing line.

(e) If a boat has one or two outstanding penalties and the other boat in her match is penalized, one penalty for each boat shall be cancelled except that a red-flag penalty shall not cancel an outstanding penalty.

(f) If a boat has more than two outstanding penalties, the umpires shall signal her disqualification under rule C5.4.

C7.3 **Penalty Limitations**

(a) A boat taking a penalty that includes a tack shall have the spinnaker head below the main-boom gooseneck from the time she passes head to wind until she is on a close-hauled course.

(b) No part of a penalty may be taken within two of a boat's hull lengths of a rounding *mark*.

(c) If a boat has one outstanding penalty, she may take the penalty any time after *starting* and before *finishing*. If a boat has two outstanding penalties, she shall take one of them as soon as reasonably possible, but not before *starting*.

(d) When the umpires display a red flag with or soon after a penalty flag, the penalized boat shall take a penalty as soon as reasonably possible, but not before *starting*.

C7.4   Taking and Completing Penalties

(a) When a boat with an outstanding penalty is on a leg to a windward *mark* and gybes, or is on a leg to a leeward *mark* or the finishing line and passes head to wind, she is taking a penalty.

(b) When a boat taking a penalty either does not take the penalty correctly or does not complete the penalty as soon as reasonably possible, she is no longer taking a penalty. The umpires shall signal this as required by rule C5.6.

(c) The umpire boat for each match shall display blue or yellow flags or shapes, each flag or shape indicating one outstanding penalty. When a boat has taken a penalty, or a penalty has been cancelled, one flag or shape shall be removed. Failure of the umpires to display or remove flags or shapes shall not change the number of penalties outstanding.

C8   PENALTIES INITIATED BY UMPIRES

C8.1   Rule Changes

(a) Rules 60.2(a) and 60.3(a) do not apply to *rules* for which penalties may be imposed by umpires.

(b) Rule 64.1(b) is changed so that the provision for exonerating a boat may be applied by the umpires without a hearing, and it takes precedence over any conflicting rule of this appendix.

C8.2

When the umpires decide that a boat has broken rule 31, 42, C4, C7.3(c) or C7.3(d) she shall be penalized by signalling her under rule C5.2 or C5.3. However, a boat that displays an incorrect flag or does not display the correct flag shall be warned orally and given an opportunity to correct the error before being penalized.

C8.3

When the umpires decide that a boat has

(a) gained an advantage by breaking a *rule* after allowing for a penalty,

(b) deliberately broken a *rule*, or

(c) committed a breach of sportsmanship, she shall be penalized under rule C5.2, C5.3 or C5.4.

C8.4

If the umpires or protest committee members decide that a boat may have broken a *rule* other than those listed in rules

C6.1(a) and C6.2, they shall so inform the protest committee for its action under rule 60.3 and rule C6.6 when appropriate.

C8.5   When, after one boat has *started*, the umpires are satisfied that the other boat will not *start*, they may signal under rule C5.4 that the boat that did not *start* is disqualified and the match is terminated.

C9   REQUESTS FOR REDRESS OR REOPENING; APPEALS; OTHER PROCEEDINGS

C9.1   There shall be no request for redress or an appeal from a decision made under rule C5, C6, C7 or C8. In rule 66 the third sentence is changed to 'A *party* to the hearing may not ask for a reopening.'

C9.2   A competitor may not base a request for redress on a claim that an action by an official boat was improper. The protest committee may decide to consider giving redress in such circumstances but only if it believes that an official boat, including an umpire boat, may have seriously interfered with a competing boat.

C9.3   No proceedings of any kind may be taken in relation to any action or non-action by the umpires, except as permitted in rule C9.2.

C10   SCORING

C10.1   The winning competitor of each match scores one point (half of one point each for a dead heat); the loser scores no points.

C10.2   When a competitor withdraws from part of an event the scores of all completed races shall stand.

C10.3   When a multiple round robin is terminated with an incomplete round robin, only one point shall be available for all the matches sailed between any two competitors, as follows:

Number of matches completed between any two competitors	*Points for each win*
1	One point
2	One-half point
3	One-third point
(etc.)	

C10.4   In a round-robin series,

(a)   competitors shall be placed in order of their total scores, highest score first;

(b)   a competitor who has won a match but is disqualified for breaking a *rule* against a competitor in another match shall lose the point for that match (but the losing competitor shall not be awarded the point); and

(c)   the overall position between competitors who have sailed in different groups shall be decided by the highest score.

C10.5   In a knockout series the sailing instructions shall state the minimum number of points required to win a series between two competitors. When a knockout series is terminated it shall be decided in favour of the competitor with the higher score.

C11   TIES

C11.1   Round-Robin Series

A round-robin series means a grouping of competitors who all sail against each other one or more times. Each separate stage identified in the event format shall be a separate round-robin series irrespective of the number of times each competitor sails against each other competitor in that stage.

Ties between two or more competitors in a round-robin series shall be broken by the following methods, in order, until all ties are broken. When one or more ties are only partially broken, rules C11.1(a) to C11.1(e) shall be reapplied to them. Ties shall be decided in favour of the competitor(s) who

(a)   placed in order, has the highest score in the matches between the tied competitors.

(b)   when the tie is between two competitors in a multiple round robin, has won the last match between the two competitors.

(c)   has the most points against the competitor placed highest in the round-robin series or, if necessary, second highest, and so on until the tie is broken. When two separate ties have to be resolved but the resolution of each depends upon resolving the other, the following principles shall be used in the rule C11.1(c) procedure:

(1)   the higher-place tie shall be resolved before the lower-place tie, and

      (2) all the competitors in the lower-place tie shall be treated as a single competitor for the purposes of rule C11.1(c).

  (d) after applying rule C10.4(c), has the highest place in the different groups, irrespective of the number of competitors in each group.

  (e) has the highest place in the most recent stage of the event (fleet race, round robin, etc.).

C11.2 Knockout Series

Ties (including 0–0) between two competitors in a knockout series shall be broken by the following methods, in order, until the tie is broken. The tie shall be decided in favour of the competitor who

  (a) has the highest place in the most recent round-robin series, applying rule C11.1 if necessary;

  (b) has won the most recent match in the event between the tied competitors.

C11.3 Remaining Ties

When rule C11.1 or C11.2 does not resolve a tie,

  (a) if the tie needs to be resolved for a later stage of the event (or another event for which the event is a direct qualifier), the tie shall be broken by a sail-off when practicable. When the race committee decides a sail-off is not practicable the tie shall be broken by a draw.

  (b) to decide the winner of an event that is not a direct qualifier for another event, or the overall position between competitors eliminated in one round of a knockout series, a sail-off may be used (but not a draw).

  (c) when a tie is not broken any monetary prizes or ranking points for tied places shall be added together and divided equally among the tied competitors.

Note: A Standard Notice of Race and Standard Sailing Instructions for match racing are available from the ISAF.

APPENDIX D – TEAM RACING RULES

Team races shall be sailed under The Racing Rules of Sailing *as changed by this appendix. If umpires will be used the sailing instructions shall so state.*

D1   CHANGES TO THE RACING RULES

D1.1   Changes to the Rules of Part 2

(a) Rule 17.2 is changed to 'Except on a beat to windward, while a boat is less than two of her hull lengths from a *leeward* boat, she shall not sail below her *proper course* unless she gybes.'

(b) The first sentence of rule 18.2(c) is changed to 'If a boat was clear ahead at the time she reached the *two-length zone*, or she later became *clear ahead* when another boat passed head to wind, the boat *clear astern* shall thereafter *keep clear*.'

(c) Rule 18.4 is deleted.

(d) Add new rule 22.3: 'A boat that has *finished* shall not act to interfere with a boat that has not *finished*.'

(e) Add new rule 22.4: 'When boats in different races meet, any change of course by either boat shall be consistent with complying with a *rule* or trying to win her own race.'

D1.2   Other Additional Rules

(a) There shall be no penalty for breaking a rule of Part 2 when the incident is between boats on the same team and there is no contact.

(b) Add to rule 41: 'However, a boat may receive help from another boat on her team provided electronic communication is not used.'

(c) A boat is not eligible for redress based on damage or injury caused by another boat on her team.

D2   PROTESTS AND PENALTIES

D2.1   Protests and Exoneration

(a) The third sentence of rule 61.1(a) and all of rule 61.1(a)(2) are deleted.

(b) A boat that, while *racing*, may have broken a rule of Part 2 (except rule 14 when she has caused damage or injury) or rule 42 may take a penalty complying with rule 44.2, except that only one turn is required.

(c) The sailing instructions may state that rule D2.4(b) applies to all *protests*.

D2.2   Umpired Races

Races to be umpired shall be identified either in the sailing instructions or by the display of flag U no later than the warning signal.

(a) When a boat protests under a rule of Part 2 or under rule 31.1, 42 or 44, she is not entitled to a hearing, except under rule 14 when there is damage or injury. Instead, when the protested boat fails either to acknowledge breaking a *rule* or to take the appropriate penalty, the protesting boat may request a decision by conspicuously displaying a yellow flag and hailing 'Umpire'.

(b) An umpire shall signal a decision as follows:

    (1) A green flag or a green and white flag means 'No penalty'.

    (2) A red flag means 'One or more boats are penalized.' The umpire shall hail or signal to identify each boat to be penalized.

(c) A boat penalized under rule D2.2(b)(2) shall take a Two-Turns Penalty under rule 44.2.

(d) PENALTIES INITIATED BY UMPIRES
When a boat

    (1) breaks rule 31.1 or 42, or a rule of Part 2 through contact with another boat on her team, and does not take a penalty;

    (2) fails to comply with rule D2.2(c);

    (3) commits a breach of sportsmanship; or

    (4) breaks rule 14 when damage or injury may have been caused;

or when a boat or her team gains an advantage despite taking a penalty, an umpire may take action without a *protest* from another boat. The umpire may impose a penalty of one or more turns, each including one tack and one gybe, signalled by displaying a red flag and hailing the boat accordingly, or report the incident to the protest committee, signalled by displaying a black flag, or both.

D2.3   Alternative Umpiring Rules

Each of these rules applies only if the sailing instructions so state.

(a) SINGLE-FLAG PROTEST PROCEDURE
Rule D2.2(a) is replaced by:
When a boat protests under a rule of Part 2 or under rule 31.1, 42 or 44, she is not entitled to a hearing, except under rule 14 when there is damage or injury. Instead, a boat involved in the incident may promptly acknowledge breaking a *rule* and take the appropriate penalty. If no boat takes a penalty, an umpire shall decide whether any boat has broken a *rule*, and shall signal the decision in compliance with rule D2.2(b).

(b) RACES WITH LIMITED UMPIRING
Rule D2.2 applies, except that when a boat complies with rule D2.2(a) and either there is no decision signalled or an umpire displays a yellow flag signalling he has insufficient facts to decide, the protesting boat is entitled to a hearing.

D2.4   Additional Protest and Redress Rules When Races Are Umpired

(a) Neither the race committee nor the protest committee shall protest a boat for breaking a rule listed in rule D2.2(a), except under rule 14 when there is damage or injury.

(b) *Protests* and requests for redress need not be in writing. The protest committee may take evidence in any way it considers appropriate and may communicate its decision orally.

(c) There shall be no request for redress or appeal by a boat arising from a decision, action or non-action by an umpire. The protest committee may decide to consider giving redress when it believes that an official boat, including an umpire boat, may have seriously interfered with a competing boat.

D3   SCORING A RACE

D3.1   (a) Each boat *finishing* a race, whether or not rule 28.1 has been complied with, shall be scored points equal to her finishing place. All other boats shall be scored points equal to the number of boats entitled to *race*.

(b) In addition, a boat's points shall be increased as follows:

Rule broken	Penalty points
Rule 28.1 when as a result she or her team has gained an advantage	10
Any other rule broken while racing for which a penalty has not been taken	6

(c) After a hearing the protest committee may penalize as follows:
  (1) When a boat has broken a *rule* and as a result her team has gained an advantage, it may increase that boat's points.
  (2) When a boat has broken rule 1 or 2, rule 14 when she has caused damage or injury, or a *rule* when not *racing*, it may penalize the boat's team by half or more race wins, or it may impose no penalty.

(d) The team with the lower total points wins the race. If the totals are equal, the team that did not have the first-place boat wins.

D3.2 When all boats on one team have *finished*, retired or failed to *start*, the race committee may stop the race. The other team's boats *racing* at that time shall be scored the points they would have received had they *finished*.

D4 SCORING A SERIES

D4.1 When two or more teams are competing in a series, the winner shall be the team scoring the greatest number of race wins. The other teams shall be ranked in order of number of race wins.

D4.2 When necessary, ties in a completed series shall be broken using, in order:

(a) the number of races won when the tied teams met;
(b) the points scored when the tied teams met;
(c) if two teams remain tied, the last race between them;
(d) total points scored in all races against common opponents;
(e) a sail-off if possible, otherwise a game of chance.

If a multiple tie is only partially resolved by one of these, then the remaining tie shall be broken by starting again at rule D4.2(a).

D4.3   If a series is not completed, teams shall be ranked according to the results from completed rounds, and ties shall be broken whenever possible using the results from races between the tied teams in the incomplete round. If no round has been completed, teams shall be ranked in order of their percentages of races won. Other ties shall be broken as provided in rule D4.2.

D5   **BREAKDOWNS WHEN BOATS ARE SUPPLIED BY THE ORGANIZING AUTHORITY**

D5.1   A supplied boat suffering a breakdown, and seeking redress as a result, shall display a red flag at the first reasonable opportunity and, if possible, continue *racing*. The race committee shall decide redress as provided in rules D5.2 and D5.3.

D5.2   When the race committee decides that the boat's finishing position was made significantly worse, that the breakdown was through no fault of the crew, and that in the same circumstances a reasonably competent crew would not have been able to avoid the breakdown, it shall make as equitable a decision as possible. This may be to order the race to be resailed or, when the boat's finishing position was predictable, award her points for that position. Any doubt about a boat's position when she broke down shall be resolved against her.

D5.3   A breakdown caused by defective supplied equipment or a breach of a *rule* by an opponent shall not normally be determined to be the fault of the crew, but one caused by careless handling, capsizing or a breach by a boat on the same team shall be. Any doubt about the fault of the crew shall be resolved in the boat's favour.

APPENDIX E – RADIO-CONTROLLED BOAT RACING RULES

Races for radio-controlled boats shall be sailed under The Racing Rules of Sailing *as changed by this appendix.*

E1 **TERMINOLOGY, RACE SIGNALS, DEFINITIONS AND FUNDAMENTAL RULES**

E1.1 **Terminology**
'Boat' means a boat that is radio-controlled by a competitor who is not on board. For 'race' used as a noun outside this appendix and outside Appendix A read 'heat'. Within this appendix, a race consists of one or more heats and is completed when the last heat in the race is finished. An 'event' consists of one or more races. A 'series' consists of a specified number of races or events.

E1.2 **Race Signals**
Delete Race Signals. All signals shall be made orally or by other sounds described in this appendix or the sailing instructions.

E1.3 **Definitions**

(a) Add to the definition *Interested Party*: 'but not a competitor when acting as an observer'.
(b) Delete the definition *Two-Length Zone* and add a new definition, *Four-Length Zone*: 'The area around a *mark* or *obstruction* within a distance of four hull lengths of the boat nearer to it.' Wherever '*two-length zone*' is used in rule 18 replace it with '*four-length zone*'.

E1.4 **Personal Buoyancy**
Rule 1.2 is changed to 'When on board a rescue boat, each competitor shall be responsible for wearing personal buoyancy adequate for the conditions.'

E1.5 **Aerials**
Transmitter aerial extremities shall be adequately protected. When a protest committee finds that a competitor has broken this rule it shall either warn him and give him time to comply or penalize him.

E2   **PART 2   WHEN BOATS MEET**
Rule 21 is changed to:

CAPSIZED OR ENTANGLED
If possible, a boat shall avoid a boat that is capsized or entangled, or has not regained control after capsizing or entanglement. A boat is capsized when her masthead is in the water. Two or more boats are entangled when lying together for a period of time so that no boat is capable of manoeuvring to break free of the other(s).

E3   **PART 3   CONDUCT OF A RACE**

E3.1   **Races with Observers**
The race committee may appoint race observers, who may be competitors. They shall remain in the control area while boats are *racing* and they shall hail and repeat the identity of boats that contact a *mark* or another boat. Such hails shall be made from the control area. Observers shall report all unresolved incidents to the race committee at the end of the heat.

E3.2   **Course Board**
Rule J2.1(4) is deleted. A course board showing the course and the limits of the control area and launching area(s) shall be located next to or within the control area with information clearly visible to competitors while *racing*.

E3.3   **Control and Launching Areas**
The control and launching area(s) shall be defined by the sailing instructions. Competitors *racing* shall remain in the control area while a heat is in progress, except that competitors may briefly go to and return from the launching area to perform functions permitted in rule E4.5. Competitors not *racing* shall remain outside the control and launching areas except when offering assistance under rule E4.2 or when acting as race observers.

E3.4   **Non-applicable Rules**
Delete the second sentence of rule 25 and all of rule 33.

E3.5   **Starting Races**
Rule 26 is changed to:

Audible signals for starting a heat shall be at one-minute

intervals and shall be a warning signal, a preparatory signal and a starting signal. During the minute before the starting signal, oral signals shall be made at ten-second intervals, and during the final ten seconds at one-second intervals. Each signal shall be timed from the beginning of its sound.

E3.6   Starting Penalties
In rules 29.1 and 30 delete the word 'crew'. Throughout rule 30 oral announcements shall be used instead of flag signals.

E3.7   Starting and Finishing Lines
The starting and finishing lines shall be tangential to, and on the course side of, the starting and finishing *marks*.

E3.8   Individual Recall
In rule 29.1 replace all after 'the race committee shall promptly' with 'twice hail "Recall (sail numbers)"'.

E3.9   General Recall
In rule 29.2 replace all after 'the race committee may' with 'twice hail "General recall" and make two loud sounds'. The warning signal for a new start for the recalled class shall be made shortly thereafter, and the starts for any succeeding classes shall follow the new start.

E3.10   Shortening or Abandoning after the Start
In rule 32.1(b) replace 'foul weather' with 'thunderstorms'. Delete rule 32.1(c).

E4   PART 4   OTHER REQUIREMENTS WHEN RACING

E4.1   Non-applicable Rules
Rules 43, 47, 48, 49, 50, 52 and 54 are deleted.

E4.2   Outside Help
Rule 41 is changed to:

(a)   A competitor shall not give tactical or strategic advice to a competitor who is *racing*.

(b)   A competitor who is *racing* shall not receive outside help except
    (1)   A boat that has gone ashore or aground outside the launching area, or become entangled with another

boat or a *mark*, may be freed and relaunched only with outside help from a rescue boat crew.

(2) Competitors who are not *racing* and others may give outside help in the launching area as permitted by rule E4.5.

E4.3   Propulsion
Rule 42 is changed so that any reference to body movement is deleted. Rule 42.3(f) is also deleted.

E4.4   Penalties for Breaking Rules of Part 2
Throughout rule 44 the penalty shall be one turn, including one tack and one gybe.

E4.5   Launching and Relaunching
Rule 45 is changed to:

(a) A boat scheduled to *race* in a heat may be launched, held on the bank, taken ashore or relaunched at any time during the heat. However, she shall not be released between the preparatory and starting signals.

(b) Boats shall be launched or recovered only from within a launching area, except as provided in rule E4.2(b)(1).

(c) While ashore or within a launching area, boats may be adjusted, drained of water or repaired; have their sails changed or reefed; have entangled objects removed; or have radio equipment repaired or changed.

E4.6   Person in Charge
In rule 46 replace 'have on board' with 'be radio-controlled by'.

E4.7   Radio

(a) A competitor shall not transmit radio signals that cause interference with the radio reception of other boats.

(b) A competitor found to have broken rule E4.7(a) shall not *race* until he has proven compliance with that rule.

E4.8   Boat Out of Radio Control
A competitor who loses radio control of his boat shall promptly hail and repeat '(The boat's sail number) out of control'. Such a boat shall be considered to have retired and shall thereafter be an *obstruction*.

E5 **PART 5 PROTESTS, REDRESS, HEARINGS, MISCON-
DUCT AND APPEALS**

E5.1 **Right to Protest; Right to Request Redress or Rule 69
Action**
Add to rule 60.1(a): 'A *protest* alleging a breach of a rule of
Part 2, 3 or 4 shall be made only by a competitor within the
control or launching area and by a boat scheduled to race in
the heat in which the incident occurred.'

E5.2 **Informing the Protestee**
In rule 61.1(a) replace all after the first sentence with 'When
her *protest* concerns an incident in the racing area that she is
involved in or sees, she shall twice hail "(Her own sail number)
protest (the sail number of the other boat)".'

E5.3 **Protest Time Limit**
In rule 61.3 replace 'two hours' with '15 minutes' and add: 'A
boat intending to protest shall also inform the race committee
within five minutes of the end of the relevant heat.'

E5.4 **Accepting Responsibility**
A boat that acknowledges breaking a rule of Part 2, 3 or 4
before the *protest* is found to be valid may retire from the relevant heat without further penalty.

E5.5 **Redress**

(a) Add to rule 62.1:
   (e) radio interference, or
   (f) an entanglement or grounding because of the
       action of a boat that was breaking a rule of Part 2
       or of a vessel not *racing* that was required to keep
       clear.
(b) In rule 62.2 replace 'two hours' with '15 minutes'.

E5.6 **Right to Be Present**
In rule 63.3(a) replace 'shall have been on board' with 'shall
have been radio-controlling them'.

E5.7 **Taking Evidence and Finding Facts**
Add to rule 63.6: 'Evidence about an alleged breach of a rule of
Part 2, 3 or 4 given by competitors shall be accepted only from
a competitor who was within the control or launching area

and whose boat was scheduled to *race* in the heat in which the incident occurred.'

E5.8   Penalties and Exoneration
When a protest committee finds that a boat has broken rule E3.3, E4.2(a) or E4.5, it shall either disqualify her from her next race or require her to make one or more penalty turns in her next race as soon as possible after *starting*.

E5.9   Decisions on Redress
Add to rule 64.2: 'If a boat given redress was damaged, she shall be given reasonable time, but not more than 30 minutes, to effect repairs before her next heat.'

E5.10   Reopening a Hearing
In rule 66 replace '24 hours' with 'ten minutes'.

E6   APPENDIX G   IDENTIFICATION ON SAILS
Appendix G is changed as follows:

(a) The text of rule G1.1 before rule G1.1(a) is changed to
       Every boat of an ISAF Radio Sailing Division (RSD) class shall display a sail number on both sides of each sail. Class insignia and national letters shall be displayed on mainsails as stated in rules G1.1(a), G1.1(b) and E6(f)(1).

(b) Rule G1.1(c) is changed to
       a sail number, which shall be the last two digits of the boat registration number or the competitor's personal number allotted by the relevant issuing authority. A single-digit number shall be prefixed with a '0'. There shall be space in front of a sail number for the prefix '1', which may be required by the race committee where there is a conflict between sail numbers. Where a conflict remains, the race committee shall require that sail numbers be suitably changed until the conflict is resolved. Any prefix '1' or other required change shall become part of the sail number.

(c) Delete the sentence after rule G1.1(c).

(d) Rule G1.2(b) is changed to
       The height of characters and distance between them on the same and opposite sides of the sail shall be as follows:

	Minimum	Maximum
Class insignia:		
Except where positioned back to back, shortest distance between insignia on opposite sides of sail	20mm	
Sail numbers:		
Height of characters	100mm	110mm
Shortest distance between adjoining characters on same side of sail	20mm	30mm
Shortest distance between sail numbers on opposite sides of sail and between sail numbers and other identification	60mm	
National letters:		
Height of characters	60mm	70mm
Shortest distance between adjoining characters on same side of sail	13mm	23mm
Shortest distance between national letters on opposite sides of sail	40mm	

(e) Rule G1.3 is changed to:

    (1) Class insignia may be positioned back to back on opposite sides of the sail where the design coincides. Otherwise class insignia, sail numbers and national letters shall be positioned at different heights, with those on the starboard side being uppermost.

    (2) On a mainsail, sail numbers shall be positioned above the national letters and below the class insignia.

    (3) Sail numbers shall be positioned on a mainsail above the line perpendicular to the luff through the quarter leech point.

(f) Where the size of a sail makes it impossible to comply with the minimum dimensions in rule E6(d) or the positioning requirements in rule E6(e)(3), exceptions are permitted in the following order of priority:

    (1) omission of national letters;

    (2) position of the mainsail sail numbers lower than the line perpendicular to the luff through the quarter leech point;

(3) reduction of the shortest distance between sail numbers on opposite sides of the sail provided the shortest
distance is not less than 20 mm;

(4) reduction of the height of sail numbers.

APPENDIX F – APPEALS PROCEDURES

*See rule 70. A national authority may change this appendix by pre-
scription but it shall not be changed by sailing instructions.*

F1   APPEALS AND REQUESTS

Appeals, requests by protest committees for confirmation or
correction of their decisions, and requests for interpretations of
the *rules* shall be made to the national authority of the venue.

F2   SUBMISSION OF DOCUMENTS

F2.1   Within 15 days of receiving the protest committee's written
decision or its decision not to reopen a hearing, the appellant
shall send an appeal and a copy of the protest committee's decision to the national authority. The appeal shall state why the
appellant believes the protest committee's decision or its procedures were incorrect.

F2.2   The appellant shall also send, with the appeal or as soon as possible thereafter, all of the following documents that are
available to her:

(a) the written *protest*(s) or request(s) for redress;

(b) a diagram, prepared or endorsed by the protest commitee,
showing the positions and tracks of all boats involved, the
course to the next *mark* and the required side, the force
and direction of the wind, and, if relevant, the depth of
water and direction and speed of any current;

(c) the notice of race, the sailing instructions, any other conditions governing the event, and any changes to them;

(d) any additional relevant documents; and

(e) the names, postal and e-mail addresses, and telephone

numbers of all *parties* to the hearing and the protest committee chairman.

F2.3   A request from a protest committee for confirmation or correction of its decision shall be sent within 15 days of the decision and shall include the decision and the documents listed in rule F2.2. A request for an interpretation of the *rules* shall include assumed facts.

F3   RESPONSIBILITIES OF NATIONAL AUTHORITY AND PROTEST COMMITTEE
Upon receipt of an appeal or a request for confirmation or correction, the national authority shall send to the *parties* and protest committee copies of the appeal or request and the protest committee's decision. It shall ask the protest committee for any relevant documents listed in rule F2.2 not sent by the appellant or the protest committee, and the protest committee shall promptly send them to the national authority. When the national authority has received them it shall send copies to the *parties*.

F4   COMMENTS
The *parties* and protest committee may make comments on the appeal or request or on any of the documents listed in rule F2.2 by sending them in writing to the national authority. Comments on any document shall be made within 15 days of receiving it from the national authority. The national authority shall send copies of the comments to the *parties* and protest committee as appropriate.

F5   INADEQUATE FACTS; REOPENING
The national authority shall accept the protest committee's finding of facts except when it decides they are inadequate. In that case it shall require the committee to provide additional facts or other information, or to reopen the hearing and report any new finding of facts, and the committee shall promptly do so.

F6   WITHDRAWING AN APPEAL
An appellant may withdraw an appeal before it is decided by accepting the protest committee's decision.

APPENDIX G – IDENTIFICATION ON SAILS

See rule 77.

G1 **ISAF INTERNATIONAL CLASS BOATS**

G1.1 **Identification**
Every boat of an ISAF International Class or Recognized Class shall carry on her mainsail and, as provided in rules G1.3(d) and G1.3(e) for letters and numbers only, on her spinnaker and headsail

(a) the insignia denoting her class;

(b) at all international events, except when the boats are provided to all competitors, national letters denoting her national authority from the table below. For the purposes of this rule, international events are ISAF events, world and continental championships, and events described as international events in their notices of race and sailing instructions; and

(c) a sail number of no more than four digits allotted by her national authority or, when so required by the class rules, by the international class association. The four-digit limitation does not apply to classes whose ISAF membership or recognition took effect before 1 April 1997. Alternatively, if permitted in the class rules, an owner may be allotted a personal sail number by the relevant issuing authority, which may be used on all his boats in that class.

Sails measured before 31 March 1999 shall comply with rule G1.1 or with the rules applicable at the time of measurement.

National Sail Letters

National authority	Letters	National authority	Letters
Algeria	ALG	Antigua	ANT
American Samoa	ASA	Argentina	ARG
Andorra	AND	Australia	AUS
Angola	ANG	Austria	AUT

National authority	Letters	National authority	Letters
Azerbaijan	AZE	Israel	ISR
Bahamas	BAH	Italy	ITA
Bahrain	BRN	Jamaica	JAM
Barbados	BAR	Japan	JPN
Belarus	BLR	Kazakhstan	KAZ
Belgium	BEL	Kenya	KEN
Bermuda	BER	Korea	KOR
Brazil	BRA	Kuwait	KUW
British Virgin Islands	IVB	Latvia	LAT
Bulgaria	BUL	Lebanon	LIB
Canada	CAN	Libya	LBA
Cayman Islands	CAY	Liechtenstein	LIE
Chile	CHI	Lithuania	LTU
China, PR	CHN	Luxembourg	LUX
Chinese Taipei	TPE	Malaysia	MAS
Columbia	COL	Malta	MLT
Cook Islands	COK	Mauritius	MRI
Croatia	CRO	Mexico	MEX
Cuba	CUB	Micronesia	FSM
Cyprus	CYP	Moldova	MDA
Czech Republic	CZE	Monaco	MON
Denmark	DEN	Morocco	MAR
Dominican Republic	DOM	Myanmar	MYA
Ecuador	ECU	Namibia	NAM
Egypt	EGY	The Netherlands	NED
El Salvador	ESA	Netherlands Antilles	AHO
Estonia	EST	New Zealand	NZL
Fiji	FIJ	Norway	NOR
Finland	FIN	Pakistan	PAK
France	FRA	Papua New Guinea	PNG
FYRO Macedonia	MKD	Paraguay	PAR
Germany	GER	Peru	PER
Great Britain	GBR	Philippines	PHI
Greece	GRE	Poland	POL
Grenada	GRN	Portugal	POR
Guam	GUM	Puerto Rico	PUR
Guatemala	GUA	Qatar	QAT
Hong Kong	HKG	Romania	ROM
Hungary	HUN	Russia	RUS
Iceland	ISL	Samoa	SAM
India	IND	San Marino	SMR
Indonesia	INA	Seychelles	SEY
Ireland	IRL	Singapore	SIN

National authority	Letters	National authority	Letters
Slovak Republic	SVK	Trinidad & Tobago	TRI
Slovenia	SLO	Tunisia	TUN
Solomon Islands	SOL	Turkey	TUR
South Africa	RSA	Ukraine	UKR
Spain	ESP	United Arab Emirates	UAE
Sri Lanka	SRI	United States of America	USA
St Lucia	LCA	Uruguay	URU
Sweden	SWE	US Virgin Islands	ISV
Switzerland	SUI	Venezuela	VEN
Tahiti	TAH	Yugoslavia	YUG
Thailand	THA	Zimbabwe	ZIM

G1.2 Specifications

(a) National letters and sail numbers shall be in capital letters and Arabic numerals, clearly legible and of the same colour. Commercially available typefaces giving the same or better legibility than Helvetica are acceptable.

(b) The height of characters and space between adjoining characters on the same and opposite sides of the sail shall be related to the boat's overall length as follows:

Overall length	Minimum height	Minimum space between characters and from edge of sail
under 3.5 m	230 mm	45 mm
3.5 m–8.5 m	300 mm	60 mm
8.5 m–11 m	375 mm	75 mm
over 11 m	450 mm	90 mm

G1.3 Positioning

Class insignia, national letters and sail numbers shall be positioned as follows:

(a) Except as provided in rules G1.3(d) and G1.3(e), class insignia, national letters and sail numbers shall when possible be wholly above an arc whose centre is the head point and whose radius is 60% of the leech length. They shall be placed at different heights on the two sides of the sail, those on the starboard side being uppermost.

(b) The class insignia shall be placed above the national let-
     ters. If the class insignia is of such a design that two of
     them coincide when placed back to back on both sides of
     the sail, they may be so placed.

(c) National letters shall be placed above the sail number.

(d) The national letters and sail number shall be displayed on
     the front side of a spinnaker but may be placed on both
     sides. They shall be displayed wholly below an arc whose
     centre is the head point and whose radius is 40% of the
     foot median and, when possible, wholly above an arc
     whose radius is 60% of the foot median.

(e) The national letters and sail number shall be displayed on
     both sides of a headsail whose clew can extend behind the
     mast 30% or more of the mainsail foot length. They shall
     be displayed wholly below an arc whose centre is the head
     point and whose radius is half the luff length and, if pos-
     sible, wholly above an arc whose radius is 75% of the luff
     length.

G2   **OTHER BOATS**
      Other boats shall comply with the rules of their national
      authority or class association in regard to the allotment, carry-
      ing and size of insignia, letters and numbers. Such rules shall,
      when practicable, conform to the above requirements.

G3   **CHARTERED OR LOANED BOATS**
      When so stated in the notice of race or sailing instructions, a
      boat chartered or loaned for an event may carry national let-
      ters or a sail number in contravention of her class rules.

G4   **WARNINGS AND PENALTIES**
      When a protest committee finds that a boat has broken a rule
      of this appendix it shall either warn her and give her time to
      comply or penalize her.

G5   **CHANGES BY CLASS RULES**
      ISAF classes may change the rules of this appendix provided
      the changes have first been approved by the ISAF.

APPENDIX H – WEIGHING CLOTHING AND EQUIPMENT

See rule 43. This appendix shall not be changed by sailing instructions or prescriptions of national authorities.

H1   Items of clothing and equipment to be weighed shall be arranged on a rack. After being saturated in water the items shall be allowed to drain freely for one minute before being weighed. The rack must allow the items to hang as they would hang from clothes hangers, so as to allow the water to drain freely. Pockets that have drain-holes that cannot be closed shall be empty, but pockets or items that can hold water shall be full.

H2   When the weight recorded exceeds the amount permitted, the competitor may rearrange the items on the rack and the measurer shall again soak and weigh them. This may be repeated a second time if the weight still exceeds the amount permitted.

H3   A competitor wearing a dry-suit may choose an alternative means of weighing the items:

   (a)   The dry-suit and items of clothing and equipment worn outside the dry-suit shall be weighed as described above.
   (b)   Clothing worn underneath the dry-suit shall be weighed as worn while *racing*, without draining.
   (c)   The two weights shall be added together.

APPENDIX J – NOTICE OF RACE AND SAILING INSTRUCTIONS

See rules 88.2(a) and 89.2. The term 'race' includes a regatta or other series of races.

J1   NOTICE OF RACE CONTENTS

J1.1   The notice of race shall include the following information:

(1) the title, place and dates of the race and name of the organizing authority;

(2) that the race will be governed by the *rules* as defined in *The Racing Rules of Sailing*;

(3) a list of any other documents that will govern the event (for example, *The Equipment Rules of Sailing*, to the extent that they apply), stating where or how each document or a copy of it may be seen;

(4) the classes to race, any handicap or rating system that will be used and the classes to which it will apply, conditions of entry and any restrictions on entries;

(5) the times of registration and warning signals for the practice race or first race, and succeeding races if known.

J1.2   The notice of race shall include any of the following that would help competitors decide whether to attend the event or that conveys other information they will need before the sailing instructions become available:

(1) identification of any racing rules that will be changed, a summary of the changes, and a statement that the changes will appear in full in the sailing instructions (see rule 86);

(2) that advertising will be restricted to Category A (see ISAF Regulation 20) and other information related to Regulation 20;

(3) that the ISAF Sailor Classification Code will apply;

(4) for an international event, any prescriptions of the national authority that may require advance preparation;

(5) the procedure for advance registration or entry, including fees and any closing dates;

(6) an entry form, to be signed by the boat's owner or owner's representative, containing words such as 'I agree to be bound by *The Racing Rules of Sailing* and by all other *rules* that govern this event';

(7) measurement procedures or requirements for measurement or rating certificates;

(8) the time and place at which the sailing instructions will be available;

(9) any changes to class rules, referring specifically to each rule and stating the change;

(10) the courses to be sailed;

(11) the penalty for breaking a rule of Part 2, other than the Two-Turns Penalty;

(12) denial of the right of appeal, subject to rule 70.4;

(13) the scoring system, if different from the Low Point System in Appendix A, the number of races scheduled and the minimum number that must be completed to constitute a series;

(14) prizes.

J2   SAILING INSTRUCTION CONTENTS

J2.1   Sailing instructions shall include the following information:

(1)   that the race will be governed by the *rules* as defined in *The Racing Rules of Sailing*;

(2)   a list of any other documents that will govern the event (for example, *The Equipment Rules of Sailing*, to the extent that they apply);

(3)   the schedule of races, the classes to race and times of warning signals for each class;

(4)   the course(s) to be sailed, or a list of *marks* from which the course will be selected and, if relevant, how courses will be signalled;

(5)   descriptions of *marks*, including starting and finishing *marks*, stating the order and side on which each is to be left and identifying all rounding marks (see rule 28.1);

(6)   descriptions of the starting and finishing lines, class flags and any special signals to be used;

(7)   the time limit, if any, for *finishing*;

(8)   the handicap or rating system to be used, if any, and the classes to which it will apply;

(9)   the scoring system, included by reference to Appendix A, to class rules or other *rules* governing the event, or stated in full. State the number of races scheduled and the minimum number that must be completed to constitute a series.

J2.2   The sailing instructions shall include those of the following that will apply:

(1)   that advertising will be restricted to Category A (see ISAF Regulation 20) and other information related to Regulation 20;

(2) that the ISAF Sailor Classification Code will apply;

(3) replacement of the relevant rules of Part 2 with the *International Regulations for Preventing Collisions at Sea* or other government right-of-way rules, the time(s) or place(s) they will apply, and any night signals to be used by the race committee;

(4) changes to the racing rules permitted by rule 86, referring specifically to each rule and stating the change (if rule 86.2 applies, state the authorization);

(5) changes to the prescriptions of the national authority (see rule 87);

(6) at an international event, a copy in English of the pre-scriptions of the national authority that will apply;

(7) changes to class rules, referring specifically to each rule and stating the change;

(8) restrictions controlling changes to boats when supplied by the organizing authority;

(9) the registration procedure;

(10) measurement or inspection procedure;

(11) location(s) of official notice board(s);

(12) procedure for changing the sailing instructions;

(13) safety requirements, such as requirements and signals for personal buoyancy, check-in at the starting area, and check-out and check-in ashore;

(14) declaration requirements;

(15) signals to be made ashore and location of signal station(s);

(16) the racing area (a chart is recommended);

(17) approximate course length and approximate length of windward legs;

(18) description of any area designated by the race committee to be an *obstruction* (see the definition Obstruction);

(19) the time limit, if any, for boats other than the first boat to *finish*;

(20) time allowances;

(21) the location of the starting area and any applicable restrictions;

(22) any special procedures or signals for individual or general recall;

(23) boats identifying *mark* locations;

(24) any special procedures or signals for changing the posi-tion of a *mark* after the start;

(25) any special procedures for shortening the course or for *fin-ishing* a shortened course;

(26) restrictions on use of support boats, plastic pools, radios, etc; on hauling out; and on outside assistance provided to a boat that is not *racing*;

(27) the penalty for breaking a rule of Part 2, other than the Two-Turns Penalty;

(28) penalization without a hearing under rule 67 for breaking rule 42;

(29) whether Appendix P will apply;

(30) protest procedure and times and place of hearings;

(31) if rule N1.4(b) will apply, the time limit for requesting a hearing under that rule;

(32) denial of the right of appeal, subject to rule 70.4;

(33) the national authority's approval of the appointment of an international jury under rule 90(b);

(34) substitution of competitors;

(35) the minimum number of boats appearing in the starting area required for a race to be started;

(36) when and where races *postponed* or *abandoned* for the day will be resailed;

(37) tides and currents;

(38) prizes;

(39) other commitments of the race committee and obligations of boats.

APPENDIX K – NOTICE OF RACE GUIDE

This guide provides a notice of race designed primarily for major championship regattas for one or more classes. It therefore will be particularly useful for world, continental and national championships and other events of similar importance. It can be downloaded from the ISAF website (www.sailing.org) as a basic text for producing a notice of race for any particular event.

The guide can also be useful for other events. However, for such events some of the paragraphs will be unnecessary or undesirable. Organizing authorities should therefore be careful in making their choices.

This guide relates closely to Appendix L, Sailing Instructions Guide, and its extended version Appendix LE on the ISAF website, the introduction to which contains principles that also apply to a notice of race.

To use this guide, first review rule J1 and decide which paragraphs will be needed. Paragraphs that are required by rule J1.1 are marked with an asterisk (*). Delete all inapplicable or unnecessary paragraphs. Select the version preferred where there is a choice. Follow the directions in the left margin to fill in the spaces where a solid line (_____) appears and select the preferred wording if a choice or option is shown in brackets ([. . .]).

After deleting unused paragraphs, renumber all paragraphs in sequential order. Be sure that paragraph numbers are correct where one paragraph refers to another.

The items listed below, when applicable, should be distributed with the notice of race, but should not be included as numbered paragraphs within the notice.

1   *An entry form, to be signed by the boat's owner or owner's representative, containing words such as 'I agree to be bound by* The Racing Rules of Sailing *and by all other rules that govern this event.'*

2   *In an international event, the applicable prescriptions of the national authority in English.*

3   *List of sponsors, if appropriate.*

4   *Lodging and camping information.*

5   *Description of meal facilities.*

6   *Race committee and [protest committee] [jury] members.*

7   *Special mooring or storage requirements.*

8   *Sail and boat repair facilities and ship's chandlers.*

9   *Charter boat availability.*

On separate lines, insert the full name of the regatta, the inclusive dates from measurement or the practice race until the final race or closing ceremony, the name of the organizing authority, and the city and country.

_____

_____

_____

_____

NOTICE OF RACE

1   RULES

1.1*   The regatta will be governed by the rules as defined in *The Racing Rules of Sailing.*

Insert the name. List by number and title the prescriptions that will apply. If the second sentence is used, state the relevant prescriptions in full.

1.2   The following prescriptions of the _____ national authority will apply [and will be stated in full in the sailing instructions]. [Of these, those that may require advance preparation are stated in full below.]

(OR)

Use only if the national authority for the venue of the event has not adopted a prescription to rule 87.

1.2   No national authority prescriptions will apply.

List by name any other documents that govern the event; for example, The Equipment Rules of Sailing, *to the extent that they apply.*

1.3*   _____ will apply.

See rule 86. Insert the rule number(s) and summarize the changes.

1.4   Racing rule(s) _____ will be changed as follows: _____. The changes will appear in full in the sailing instructions.

Inform competitors of proper changes. Insert the rule number(s) and class name. Make a separate statement for the rules of each class.

1.5   Rule(s) _____ of the _____ class rules [will not apply] [is (are) changed as follows: _____].

1.6   If there is a conflict between languages the English text will take precedence.

See ISAF Regulation 20. Include other applicable information related to Regulation 20.

2 **ADVERTISING**
Advertising will be restricted to Category A.

3* **ELIGIBILITY AND ENTRY**

Insert the class(es).

3.1 The regatta is open to all boats of the _____ class(es).

(OR)

Insert the class(es) and eligibility requirements.

3.1 The regatta is open to boats of the _____ class(es) that _____.

Insert the postal, fax and e-mail addresses and entry closing date.

3.2 Eligible boats may enter by completing the attached form and sending it, together with the required fee, to _____ by _____.

Insert any conditions.

3.3 Late entries will be accepted under the following conditions: _____.

Insert any restrictions.

3.4 The following restrictions on the number of boats apply: _____.

4 **CLASSIFICATION**
The ISAF Sailor Classification Code will apply.

5 **FEES**

Insert all required fees for racing.

5.1 Required fees are as follows:

Class	Fee
_____	_____
_____	_____
_____	_____

Insert optional fees (eg for social events).

5.2 Other fees:

_____

_____

Use only when a class is divided into fleets racing a qualifying series and a final series.

6   QUALIFYING SERIES AND FINAL SERIES

The regatta will consist of a qualifying series and a final series.

7   SCHEDULE

Insert the day, date and times.

7.1*   Registration:

Day and date _____

From _____   To _____

Insert the day, date and times.

7.2   Measurement and inspection:

Day and date _____

From _____   To _____

Revise as desired and insert the dates and classes. Include a practice race if any. When the series consists of qualifying races and final races, specify them. The schedule can also be given in an attachment.

7.3*   Dates of racing:

Date	Class _____	Class _____
_____	racing	racing
_____	racing	reserve day
_____	reserve day	racing
_____	racing	racing
_____	racing	racing

Insert the classes and numbers.

7.4   Number of races:

Class	Number	Races per day
_____	_____	_____
_____	_____	_____

Insert the time.

7.5*   The scheduled time of the warning signal for the [practice race] [first race] [each day] is _____.

8   MEASUREMENTS

Each boat shall produce a valid [measurement] [rating] certificate.

(OR)

List the measurements with appropriate references to the class rules.

Each boat shall produce a valid [measurement] [rating] certificate. In addition the following measurements [may] [will] be taken: _____.

9 SAILING INSTRUCTIONS

Insert the time, date and location.

The sailing instructions will be available after _____ on _____ at _____.

10 VENUE

Insert a number or letter. Provide a marked map with driving instructions.

10.1 Attachment _____ shows the location of the regatta harbour.

Insert a number or letter. Provide a marked map or chart.

10.2 Attachment _____ shows the location of the racing areas.

11 THE COURSES

Include the description.

The courses to be sailed will be as follows: _____.

(OR)

Insert a number or letter. A method of illustrating various courses is shown in Addendum A of Appendix L or LE. Insert the course length if applicable.

The diagrams in Attachment _____ show the courses, including the approximate angles between legs, the order in which marks are to be passed, and the side on which each mark is to be left. [The approximate course length will be _____.]

12 PENALTY SYSTEM

Include paragraph 12.1 only when the Two-Turns Penalty will not be used. Insert the number of places or describe the penalties.

12.1 The Scoring Penalty, rule 44.3, will apply. The penalty will be _____ places.

(OR)

12.1 The penalties are as follows: _____.

Insert the class(es).

12.2 For the _____ class(es) rules 44.1 and 44.2 are changed so that only one turn, including one tack and one gybe, is required.

Include only if the protest committee is an international jury or another provision of rule 70.4 applies. Use 'jury' only if referring to an international jury.

12.3 Decisions of the [protest committee] [jury] will be final as provided in rule 70.4.

13   SCORING

Include only if the Low Point System is replaced by the Bonus Point System.

13.1 The Bonus Point System of Appendix A will apply.

(OR)

Include only if neither of the Appendix A scoring systems will be used. Describe the system.

13.1 The scoring system is as follows: _____.

Insert the number.

13.2 _____ races are required to be completed to constitute a series.

Insert the numbers throughout.

13.3 (a) When fewer than _____ races have been completed, a boat's series score will be the total of her race scores.

(b) When from _____ to _____ races have been completed, a boat's series score will be the total of her race scores excluding her worst score.

(c) When _____ or more races have been completed, a boat's series score will be the total of her race scores excluding her two worst scores.

Insert the identification markings. National letters are suggested for international events.

14   SUPPORT BOATS
Support boats shall be marked with _____.

15   BERTHING
Boats shall be kept in their assigned places in the [boat park] [harbour].

16 **HAUL-OUT RESTRICTIONS**
Keel boats shall not be hauled out during the regatta except with and according to the terms of prior written permission of the race committee.

17 **DIVING EQUIPMENT AND PLASTIC POOLS**
Underwater breathing apparatus and plastic pools or their equivalent shall not be used around keel boats between the preparatory signal of the first race and the end of the regatta.

Insert any alternative text that applies. Describe the radio communication bands or frequencies that will be used or allowed.

18 **RADIO COMMUNICATION**
A boat shall neither make radio transmissions while racing nor receive radio communications not available to all boats. This restriction also applies to mobile telephones.

When perpetual trophies will be awarded state their complete names.

19 **PRIZES**
Prizes will be given as follows: _____.

20 **DISCLAIMER OF LIABILITY**
Competitors participate in the regatta entirely at their own risk. See rule 4, Decision to Race. The organizing authority will not accept any liability for material damage or personal injury or death sustained in conjunction with or prior to, during, or after the regatta.

Insert the currency and amount.

21 **INSURANCE**
Each participating boat shall be insured with valid third-party liability insurance with a minimum cover of _____ per event or the equivalent.

Insert necessary contact information: person or organization, address, telephone, fax, e-mail.

22 **FURTHER INFORMATION**
For further information please contact _____.

APPENDIX L – SAILING INSTRUCTIONS GUIDE

This guide provides a set of tested sailing instructions designed primarily for major championship regattas for one or more classes. It therefore will be particularly useful for world, continental and national championships and other events of similar importance. The guide can also be useful for other events; however, for such events some of these instructions will be unnecessary or undesirable. Race officers should therefore be careful in making their choices.

An expanded version of the guide, Appendix LE, is available on the ISAF website (www.sailing.org). It contains provisions applicable to the largest and most complicated multi-class events, as well as variations on several of the sailing instructions recommended in this appendix. It will be revised from time to time, to reflect advances in race management techniques as they develop, and can be downloaded as a basic text for producing the sailing instructions for any particular event. Appendix L can also be downloaded from the ISAF website.

The principles on which all sailing instructions should be based are as follows:

1   *They should include only two types of statement: the intentions of the race committee and the obligations of competitors.*
2   *They should be concerned only with racing. Information about social events, assignment of moorings, etc., should be provided separately.*
3   *They should not change the racing rules except when clearly desirable.*
4   *They should not repeat or restate any of the racing rules.*
5   *They should not repeat themselves.*
6   *They should be in chronological order; that is, the order in which the competitor will use them.*
7   *They should, when possible, use words or phrases from the racing rules.*

To use this guide, first review rule J2 and decide which instructions will be needed. Instructions that are required by rule J2.1 are marked with an asterisk (*). Delete all inapplicable or unnecessary instructions. Select the version preferred where there is a choice.

Follow the directions in the left margin to fill in the spaces where a solid line (_____) appears and select the preferred wording if a choice or option is shown in brackets ([. . .]).

After deleting unused instructions, renumber all instructions in sequential order. Be sure that instruction numbers are correct where one instruction refers to another.

On separate lines, insert the full name of the regatta, the inclusive dates from measurement or the practice race until the final race or closing ceremony, the name of the organizing authority, and the city and country.

_____

_____

_____

_____

Sailing Instructions

1   RULES

1.1*   The regatta will be governed by the rules as defined in *The Racing Rules of Sailing*.

Insert the name. State the relevant prescriptions in full.

1.2   The following prescriptions of the _____ national authority will apply: _____.

(OR)

Use only if the national authority for the venue of the event has not adopted a prescription to rule 87.

1.2   No national authority prescriptions will apply.

List by name any other documents that govern the event; for example, The Equipment Rules of Sailing, to the extent that they apply.

1.3*   _____ will apply.

See rule 86. Insert the rule number(s) and state the changes.

1.4   Racing rule(s) _____ will be changed as follows: _____.

Insert the rule number(s) and class name. Make a separate statement for the rules of each class.

1.5   Rule(s) _____ of the _____ class rules [will not apply] [is (are) changed as follows: _____].

1.6   If there is a conflict between languages the English text will take precedence.

Insert the location(s).

2   NOTICES TO COMPETITORS

Notices to competitors will be posted on the official notice board(s) located at _____.

Change the times if different.

3   CHANGES TO SAILING INSTRUCTIONS

Any change to the sailing instructions will be posted before 0900 on the day it will take effect, except that any change to the schedule of races will be posted by 2000 on the day before it will take effect.

4   SIGNALS MADE ASHORE

Insert the location.

4.1   Signals made ashore will be displayed at _____.

Insert the number of minutes.

4.2   When flag AP is displayed ashore, '1 minute' is replaced with 'not less than _____ minutes' in the race signal AP.

(OR)

Insert the number of minutes.

4.2   Flag D with a sound means 'The warning signal will be made not less than _____ minutes after flag D is displayed. [Boats are requested not to leave the harbour until this signal is made.]'

Delete if a class rule applies.

4.3   When flag Y is displayed ashore, rule 40.1 applies at all times while afloat. This changes the Part 4 preamble.

5 SCHEDULE OF RACES

Revise as desired and insert the dates and classes. Include a practice race if any. When the series consists of qualifying races and final races, specify them. The schedule can also be given in an attachment.

5.1* Dates of racing:

Date	Class _____	Class _____
_____	racing	racing
_____	racing	reserve day
_____	reserve day	racing
_____	racing	racing
_____	racing	racing

Insert the classes and numbers.

5.2* Number of races:

Class day	Number	Races per
_____	_____	_____
_____	_____	_____

(a) Reserve days may be used if races are not completed as scheduled or if the race committee considers it unlikely that races will be completed as scheduled.

(b) One extra race per day may be sailed, provided that no class becomes more than one race ahead of schedule.

Insert the time.

5.3* The scheduled time of the warning signal for the first race each day is _____.

5.4 When there has been a long postponement and when more than one race (or sequence of races, for two or more classes) will be held on the same day, the warning signal for the first race and each succeeding race will be made as soon as practicable.

To alert boats that a race or sequence of races will begin soon, an orange flag will be displayed with one sound for at least four minutes before a warning signal is displayed.

Insert the time.

5.5 On the last day of the regatta no warning signal will be made after _____.

Insert the classes and names or descriptions of the flags.

6* **CLASS FLAGS**

Class flags will be:

Class	Flag
_____	_____
_____	_____
_____	_____

Insert a number or letter.

7 **RACING AREAS**

Attachment _____ shows the location of racing areas.

8 **THE COURSES**

Insert a number or letter. A method of illustrating various courses is shown in Addendum A. Insert the course length if applicable.

8.1* The diagrams in Attachment _____ show the courses, including the approximate angles between legs, the order in which marks are to be passed, and the side on which each mark is to be left. [The approx-imate course length will be _____.]

8.2 No later than the warning signal, the race committee signal boat will display the approx-imate compass bearing of the first leg.

8.3 When there is a gate, boats shall sail between the gate marks from the direction of the previous mark and round either gate mark.

8.4 Courses will not be shortened. This changes rule 32.

Include only when changing positions of marks is impracticable.

8.5 Legs of the course will not be changed after the preparatory signal. This changes rule 33.

9 MARKS

Change the mark numbers as needed and insert the descriptions of the marks. Use the second alternative when Marks 4S and 4P form a gate, with Mark 4S to be left to starboard and Mark 4P to port. Unless clear from the course diagrams, state which marks are rounding marks.

9.1* Marks 1, 2, 3 and 4 will be _____.

(OR)

9.1* Marks 1, 2, 3, 4S and 4P will be _____.

Insert the descriptions of the marks.

9.2 New marks, as provided in instruction 12.1, will be _____.

Describe the starting and finishing marks: for example, the race committee signal boat at the starboard end and a buoy at the port end. Instruction 11.2 will describe the starting line and instruction 13 the finishing line.

9.3* The starting and finishing marks will be _____.

9.4 A race committee boat signalling a change of a leg of the course is a mark as provided in instruction 12.2.

Describe each area by its location and any easily recognized details of appearance.

10 AREAS THAT ARE OBSTRUCTIONS

The following areas are designated as obstructions: _____.

11 THE START

Include only if the asterisked option in rule 26 will be used. Insert the number of minutes.

11.1 Races will be started by using rule 26 with the warning signal given _____ minutes before the starting signal.

(OR)

For large fleets and long starting lines.

11.1 Races will be started by using rule 26 with the following addition:
An attention signal (flag F with one sound) will be made five minutes before the warning

signal for the first class to start. The race committee will designate the course to be sailed before or with the attention signal. Flag F will be removed with one sound one minute before the warning signal. This changes rule 27.1.

(OR)

Describe any starting system other than that stated in rule 26.

11.1 Races will be started as follows: _____. This changes rule 26.

11.2* The starting line will be between staffs displaying orange flags on the starting marks.

(OR)

11.2* The starting line will be between a staff displaying an orange flag on the starting mark at the starboard end and the port-end starting mark.

(OR)

Insert the description.

11.2* The starting line will be _____.

11.3 Boats whose warning signal has not been made shall avoid the starting area.

Insert the number of minutes.

11.4 A boat starting later than _____ minutes after her starting signal will be scored Did Not Start. This changes rule A4.

11.5 If any part of a boat's hull, crew or equipment is on the course side of the starting line during the two minutes before her starting signal, the race committee will display flag V. It will be displayed until all boats have sailed completely to the pre-start side, but not after the starting signal.

(OR)

Insert the channel number.

11.5 If any part of a boat's hull, crew or equipment is on the course side of the starting

line during the two minutes before her starting signal and she is identified, the race
committee will attempt to broadcast her sail
number on VHF channel -_____. Failure to
make a broadcast or to time it accurately will
not be grounds for a request for redress. This
changes rule 62.1(a).

**12   CHANGE OF THE NEXT LEG OF THE
COURSE**

12.1 To change the next leg of the course, the race
committee will move the original mark (or the
finishing line) to a new position.

(OR)

12.1 To change the next leg of the course, the race
committee will lay a new mark (or move the
finishing line) and remove the original mark
as soon as practicable. When in a subsequent
change a new mark is replaced, it will be
replaced by an original mark.

*Reverse 'port' and
'starboard' when the
mark is to be left to
starboard.*

12.2 Except at a gate, boats shall pass between the
race committee boat signalling the change of
the next leg and the nearby mark, leaving the
mark to port and the race committee boat to
starboard. This changes rule 28.1.

13* THE FINISH
The finishing line will be between staffs displaying orange flags on the finishing marks.

(OR)

The finishing line will be between a staff displaying an orange flag on the finishing mark
at the starboard end and the port-end finishing mark.

(OR)

*Insert the
description.*

The finishing line will be _____.

14   PENALTY SYSTEM

Include instruction 14.1 only when the Two-Turns Penalty will not be used. Insert the number of places or describe the penalties.

14.1 The Scoring Penalty, rule 44.3, will apply. The penalty will be _____ places.

(OR)

Insert the class(es).

14.1 The penalties are as follows: _____.

14.2 For the _____ class(es) rules 44.1 and 44.2 are changed so that only one turn, including one tack and one gybe, is required.

14.3 A boat that has taken a penalty under rule 31.2 or 44.1 shall complete an acknowledgment form at the race office within the protest time limit.

Here and below, use 'jury' only when referring to an international jury.

14.4 As provided in rule 67, the [protest committee] [jury] may, without a hearing, penalize a boat that has broken rule 42.

(OR)

14.4 Appendix P will apply [as changed by instruction(s)] [14.2] [and] [14.5].

Recommended only for junior events.

14.5 Rule P2.3 will not apply and rule P2.2 is changed so that it will apply to any protest after the first one.

15   TIME LIMITS

Insert the classes and times. Omit the Mark 1 time limit if inapplicable.

15.1*Time limits are as follows:

Class	Time limit	Mark 1 time limit
_____	_____	_____
_____	_____	_____
_____	_____	_____

If no boat has passed Mark 1 within the Mark 1 time limit the race will be abandoned.

Insert the time (or different times for different classes).

15.2 Boats failing to finish within _____ after the first boat sails the course and finishes will be scored Did Not Finish. This changes rules 35 and A4.

16 **PROTESTS AND REQUESTS FOR REDRESS**

16.1 Protest forms are available at the race office. Protests shall be delivered there within the protest time limit.

Change the time if different.

16.2 For each class, the protest time limit is 90 minutes after the last boat has finished the last race of the day. [The same time limit applies to protests by the race committee and [protest committee] [jury] about incidents they observe in the racing area and to requests for redress. This changes rules 61.3 and 62.2.]

Change the posting time if different. Insert the jury room location and the time for the first hearing.

16.3 Notices will be posted within 30 minutes of the protest time limit to inform competitors of hearings in which they are parties or named as witnesses. Hearings will be held in the jury room, located at _____, beginning at _____.

16.4 Notices of protests by the race committee or [protest committee] [jury] will be posted to inform boats under rule 61.1(b).

16.5 A list of boats that, under instruction 14.4, have acknowledged breaking rule 42 or have been disqualified by the [protest committee] [jury] will be posted before the protest time limit.

16.6 Breaches of instructions 11.3, 14.3, 18, 19.2, 22, 23 and 24 will not be grounds for a protest by a boat. This changes rule 60.1(a). Penalties for these breaches may be less than disqualification if the [protest committee] [jury] so decides.

16.7 On the last day of the regatta a request for reopening a hearing shall be delivered

(a) within the protest time limit if the party requesting reopening was informed of the decision on the previous day;

Change the time if different.

(b) no later than 30 minutes after the party requesting reopening was informed of the decision on that day.

This changes rule 66.

Include only if the protest committee is an international jury or another provision of rule 70.4 applies.

16.8 Decisions of the [protest committee] [jury] will be final as provided in rule 70.4.

17   SCORING

Include only if the Low Point System is replaced by the Bonus Point System.

17.1*The Bonus Point System of Appendix A will apply.

(OR)

Include only if neither of the Appendix A scoring systems will be used. Describe the system.

17.1*The scoring system is as follows: _____.

Insert the number.

17.2*_____ races are required to be completed to constitute a series.

Insert the numbers throughout.

17.3 (a) When fewer than _____ races have been completed, a boat's series score will be the total of her race scores.

(b) When from _____ to _____ races have been completed, a boat's series score will be the total of her race scores excluding her worst score.

(c) When _____ or more races have been completed, a boat's series score will be the total of her race scores excluding her two worst scores.

18   SAFETY REGULATIONS

Insert the procedure for check-out and check-in.

18.1 Check-out and check-in: _____.

18.2 A boat that retires from a race shall notify the race committee as soon as possible.

19 REPLACEMENT OF CREW OR EQUIPMENT

19.1 Substitution of competitors will not be allowed without prior written approval of the [race committee] [protest committee] [jury].

19.2 Substitution of damaged or lost equipment will not be allowed unless approved by the race committee. Requests for substitution shall be made to the committee at the first reasonable opportunity.

20 EQUIPMENT AND MEASUREMENT CHECKS

A boat or equipment may be inspected at any time for compliance with the class rules and sailing instructions. On the water, a boat can be instructed by a race committee measurer to proceed immediately to a designated area for inspection.

Insert the descriptions. If appropriate, use different identification markings for boats performing different duties.

21 OFFICIAL BOATS

Official boats will be marked as follows: _____.

22 SUPPORT BOATS

22.1 Team leaders, coaches and other support personnel shall stay outside areas where boats are racing from the time of the preparatory signal for the first class to start until all boats have finished or the race committee signals a postponement, general recall or abandonment.

Insert the identification markings. National letters are suggested for international events.

22.2 Support boats shall be marked with _____.

23 HAUL-OUT RESTRICTIONS

Keel boats shall not be hauled out during the regatta except with and according to the terms of prior written permission of the race committee.

24   DIVING EQUIPMENT AND PLASTIC POOLS

Underwater breathing apparatus and plastic pools or their equivalent shall not be used around keel boats between the preparatory signal of the first race and the end of the regatta.

Insert any alternative text that applies. Describe the radio communication bands or frequencies that will be used or allowed.

25   RADIO COMMUNICATION

A boat shall neither make radio transmissions while racing nor receive radio communications not available to all boats. This restriction also applies to mobile telephones.

If perpetual trophies will be awarded state their complete names.

26   PRIZES

Prizes will be given as follows: _____.

27   DISCLAIMER OF LIABILITY

Competitors participate in the regatta entirely at their own risk. See rule 4, Decision to Race. The organizing authority will not accept any liability for material damage or personal injury or death sustained in conjunction with or prior to, during, or after the regatta.

Insert the currency and amount.

28   INSURANCE

Each participating boat shall be insured with valid third-party liability insurance with a minimum cover of _____ per event or the equivalent.

Addendum A – Illustrating The Course

Shown here are diagrams of course shapes. Any course can be similarly shown. When there is more than one course, prepare a separate diagram for each course and state how each will be signalled.

A Windward-Leeward Course

Start – 1 – 2 – 1 – 2 – Finish

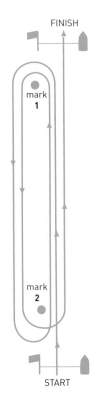

Options for this course include:
(1) increasing or decreasing the number of laps,
(2) deleting the final windward leg,
(3) using a gate instead of a leeward mark,
(4) using an offset mark at the windward mark, and
(5) using the leeward and windward marks as starting and finishing marks.

A Windward-Leeward-Triangle Course

Start – 1 – 2 – 3 – 1 – 3 – Finish

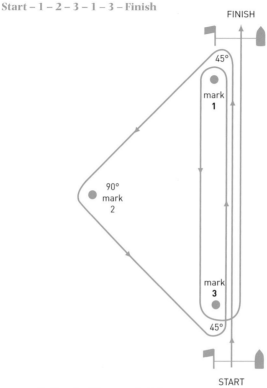

Options for this course include:

(1) *increasing or decreasing the number of laps,*

(2) *deleting the last windward leg,*

(3) *varying the interior angles of the triangle (45°–90°–45° and 60°–60°–60° are common),*

(4) *using a gate instead of a leeward mark for downwind legs (but not reaches),*

(5) *using an offset mark at the beginning of downwind legs (but not reaches), and*

(6) *using the leeward and windward marks as starting and finishing marks.*

Be sure to specify the interior angle at each mark.

Trapezoid Courses

Start – 1 – 2 – 3 – 2 – 3 – Finish

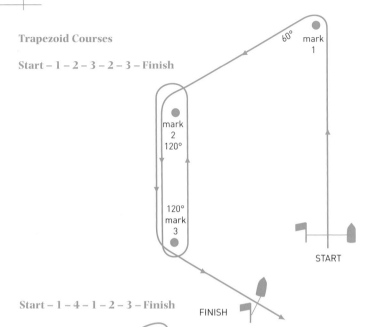

Start – 1 – 4 – 1 – 2 – 3 – Finish

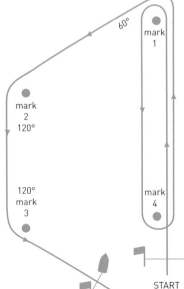

Options for these courses include:

(1) adding additional legs,

(2) using gates instead of lee-ward marks for downwind legs (but not reaches),

(3) varying the interior angles of the reaching legs,

(4) using an offset mark at the beginning of downwind legs (but not reaches), and

(5) finishing boats upwind rather than on a reach.

Be sure to specify the interior angle of each reaching leg. It is recommended that Mark 4 be different from the starting mark.

Addendum B – Boats Provided by the Organizing Authority

The following sailing instruction is recommended when all boats will be provided by the organizing authority. It can be changed to suit the circumstances. When used, it should be inserted after instruction 3.

4   BOATS

4.1   Boats will be provided for all competitors, who shall not modify them or cause them to be modified in any way except that

    (a)   a compass may be tied or taped to the hull or spars;

    (b)   wind indicators, including yarn or thread, may be tied or taped anywhere on the boat;

    (c)   hulls, centreboards and rudders may be cleaned, but only with water;

    (d)   adhesive tape may be used anywhere above the water line; and

    (e)   all fittings or equipment designed to be adjusted may be adjusted, provided that the class rules are complied with.

4.2   All equipment provided with the boat for sailing purposes shall be in the boat while afloat.

4.3   The penalty for not complying with one of the above instructions will be disqualification from all races sailed in which the instruction was broken.

4.4   Competitors shall report any damage or loss of equipment, however slight, to the organizing authority's representative immediately after securing the boat ashore. The penalty for breaking this instruction, unless the [protest committee] [jury] is satisfied that the competitor made a determined effort to comply, will be disqualification from the race most recently sailed.

4.5   Class rules requiring competitors to be members of the class association will not apply.

APPENDIX M – RECOMMENDATIONS FOR PROTEST COMMITTEES

This appendix is advisory only; in some circumstances changing these procedures may be advisable. It is addressed primarily to protest committee chairmen but may also help judges, jury secretaries, race committees and others connected with protest and redress hearings.

In a protest or redress hearing, the protest committee should weigh all testimony with equal care; should recognize that honest testimony can vary, and even be in conflict, as a result of different observations and recollections; should resolve such differences as best it can; should recognize that no boat or competitor is guilty until a breach of a *rule* has been established to the satisfaction of the protest committee; and should keep an open mind until all the evidence has been heard as to whether a boat or competitor has broken a *rule*.

M1 PRELIMINARIES (may be performed by race office staff)

- Receive the *protest* or request for redress.
- Note on the form the time the *protest* or request is delivered and the protest time limit.
- Inform each *party*, and the race committee when necessary, when and where the hearing will be held.

M2 BEFORE THE HEARING
Make sure that:

- Each *party* has a copy of or the opportunity to read the *protest* or request for redress and has had reasonable time to prepare for the hearing.
- No member of the protest committee is an *interested party*. Ask the *parties* whether they object to any member. When redress is requested under rule 62.1(a), a member of the race committee should not be a member of the protest committee.
- Only one person from each boat (or *party*) is present unless an interpreter is needed.

- All boats and people involved are present. If they are not, however, the committee may proceed under rule 63.3(b).
- Boats' representatives were on board when required (rule 63.3(a)). When the *parties* were in different races, both organizing authorities must accept the composition of the *protest* committee (rule 63.8). In a measurement protest obtain the current class rules and identify the authority responsible for interpreting them (rule 64.3(b)).

M3   THE HEARING

M3.1   Check the validity of the *protest* or request for redress.

- Are the contents adequate (rule 61.2 or 62.1)?
- Was it delivered in time? If not, is there good reason to extend the time limit (rule 61.3 or 62.2)?
- When required, was the protestor involved in or a witness to the incident (rule 60.1(a))?
- When necessary, was 'Protest' hailed and, if required, a red flag displayed correctly (rule 61.1(a))?
- When the flag and hail were not necessary was the protestee informed?
- Decide whether the *protest* or request for redress is valid (rule 63.5).
- Once the validity of the *protest* or request has been determined, do not let the subject be introduced again unless truly new evidence is available.

M3.2   Take the evidence (rule 63.6).

- Ask the protestor and then the protestee to tell their stories. Then allow them to question one another. In a redress matter, ask the *party* to state the request.
- Invite questions from protest committee members.
- Make sure you know what facts each *party* is alleging before calling any witnesses. Their stories may be different.
- Allow anyone, including a boat's crew, to give evidence. It is the *party* who normally decides which witnesses to call, although the protest committee may also call witnesses (rule 63.6). The question asked by a *party* 'Would you like to hear N?' is best answered by 'It is your choice.'
- Call each *party's* witnesses (and the protest committee's if any) one by one. Limit *parties* to questioning the witness(es) (they may wander into general statements).

- Invite the protestee to question the protestor's witness first (and vice versa). This prevents the protestor from leading his witness from the beginning.
- Allow a member of the protest committee who saw the incident to give evidence (rule 63.6) but only in the presence of the *parties*. The member may be questioned and may remain in the room (rule 63.3(a)).
- Try to prevent leading questions or hearsay evidence, but if that is impossible discount the evidence so obtained.
- Accept written evidence from a witness who is not available to be questioned only if all *parties* agree. In doing so they forego their rights to question that witness (rule 63.6).
- Ask one member of the committee to note down evidence, particularly times, distances, speeds, etc.
- Invite first the protestor and then the protestee to make a final statement of her case, particularly on any application or interpretation of the *rules*.

M3.3   Find the facts (rule 63.6).

- Write down the facts; resolve doubts one way or the other.
- Call back *parties* for more questions if necessary.
- When appropriate, draw a diagram of the incident using the facts you have found.

M3.4   Decide the *protest* or request for redress (rule 64).

- Base the decision on the facts found (if you cannot, find some more facts).
- In redress cases, make sure that no further evidence is needed from boats that will be affected by the decision.

M3.5   Inform the *parties* (rule 65).

- Recall the *parties* and read them the facts found, conclusions and *rules* that apply, and the decision. When time presses it is permissible to read the decision and give the details later.
- Give any *party* a copy of the decision on request. File the *protest* or request for redress with the committee records.

M4   **REOPENING A HEARING (rule 66)**
When a *party*, within the time limit, has asked for a hearing to be reopened, hear the *party* making the request, look at any

video, etc., and decide whether there is any material new evidence that might lead you to change your decision. Decide whether your interpretation of the *rules* may have been wrong; be open-minded as to whether you have made a mistake. If none of these applies refuse to reopen; otherwise schedule a hearing.

M5   GROSS MISCONDUCT (rule 69)

M5.1   An action under this rule is not a *protest*, but the protest committee gives its allegations in writing to the competitor before the hearing. The hearing is conducted under the same rules as other hearings but the protest committee must have at least three members (rule 69.1(b)). Use the greatest care to protect the competitor's rights.

M5.2   A competitor or a boat cannot protest under rule 69, but the protest form of a competitor who tries to do so may be accepted as a report to the protest committee, which can then decide whether or not to call a hearing.

M5.3   When it is desirable to call a hearing under rule 69 as a result of a Part 2 incident, it is important to hear any boat-vs.-boat *protest* in the normal way, deciding which boat, if any, broke which *rule*, before proceeding against the competitor under this rule.

M5.4   Although action under rule 69 is taken against a competitor, not a boat, a boat may also be penalized (rule 69.1(b)).

M5.5   The protest committee may warn the competitor (rule 69.1(b)), in which case no report is to be made to national authorities (rule 69.1(c)). When a penalty is imposed and a report is made to national authorities, it may be helpful to recommend whether or not further action should be taken.

M6   APPEALS (rule 70 and Appendix F)
When decisions can be appealed,

- retain the papers relevant to the hearing so that the information can easily be used for an appeal. Is there a diagram endorsed or prepared by the protest committee? Are the facts found sufficient? (Example: Was there an *overlap*? Yes or No. 'Perhaps' is not a fact found.) Are the names of the protest committee members and other important information on the form?

● Comments by the protest committee on any appeal should enable the appeals committee to picture the whole incident clearly; the appeals committee knows nothing about the situation.

M7 PHOTOGRAPHIC EVIDENCE

Photographs and videotapes can sometimes provide useful evidence but protest committees should recognize their limitations and note the following points:

● The *party* producing the photographic evidence is responsible for arranging the viewing.

● View the tape several times to extract all the information from it.

● The depth perception of any single-lens camera is very poor; with a telephoto lens it is non-existent. When the camera views two *overlapped* boats at right angles to their course, it is impossible to assess the distance between them. When the camera views them head on, it is impossible to see whether an *overlap* exists unless it is substantial.

● Ask the following questions:
  – Where was the camera in relation to the boats?
  – Was the camera's platform moving? If so in what direction and how fast?
  – Is the angle changing as the boats approach the critical point? Fast panning causes radical change.
  – Did the camera have an unrestricted view throughout?

APPENDIX N – INTERNATIONAL JURIES

See rules 70.4 and 90(b). This appendix shall not be changed by sailing instructions or prescriptions of national authorities.

N1 COMPOSITION, APPOINTMENT AND ORGANIZATION

N1.1 An international jury shall be composed of experienced sailors with excellent knowledge of the racing rules and extensive protest committee experience. It shall be independent of and have no members from the race committee, and be appointed by the organizing authority, subject to approval by the national authority if required (see rule 90(b)), or by the ISAF under rule 88.2(b).

N1.2   The jury shall consist of a chairman, a vice chairman if desired, and other members for a total of at least five. A majority shall be International Judges. The jury may appoint a secretary, who shall not be a member of the jury.

N1.3   No more than two members (three, in Groups M, N and Q) shall be from the same national authority.

N1.4   (a)   A jury of ten or more members may divide itself into two or more panels of at least five members each, of which the majority shall be International Judges. If this is done, the requirements for membership of a full jury shall apply to each panel but not to the jury as a whole.

   (b)   A jury of fewer than ten members may divide itself into two or three panels of at least three members each, of which the majority shall be International Judges. Members of each panel shall be from at least three different national authorities except in Groups M, N and Q, where they shall be from at least two different national authorities. If dissatisfied with a panel's decision, a *party* is entitled to a hearing by a jury composed in compliance with rules N1.1, N1.2 and N1.3, except concerning the facts found, if requested within the time limit specified in the sailing instructions.

N1.5   When a full jury has fewer than five members, because of illness or emergency, and no qualified replacements are available, it remains properly constituted if it consists of at least three members. At least two members shall be International Judges. When there are three or four members they shall be from at least three different national authorities except in Groups M, N and Q, where they shall be from at least two different national authorities.

N1.6   When the national authority's approval is required for the appointment of an international jury (see rule 90(b)), notice of its approval shall be included in the sailing instructions or be posted on the official notice board.

N1.7   If the jury acts while not properly constituted, the jury's decisions may be appealed.

N2   RESPONSIBILITIES

N2.1   An international jury is responsible for hearing and deciding all *protests*, requests for redress and other matters arising under the rules of Part 5. When asked by the organizing authority or the race committee, it shall advise and assist them on any matter directly affecting the fairness of the competition.

N2.2   Unless the organizing authority directs otherwise, the jury shall

(a)   decide questions of eligibility, measurement or boat certificates; and

(b)   authorize the substitution of competitors, boats, sails or equipment.

N2.3   If so directed by the organizing authority, the jury shall

(a)   make or approve changes to the sailing instructions,

(b)   supervise or direct the race committee in the conduct of the races, and

(c)   decide on other matters referred to it by the organizing authority.

N3   PROCEDURES

N3.1   Decisions of the jury shall be made by a simple majority vote of all members. When there is an equal division of votes cast, the chairman of the meeting may cast an additional vote.

N3.2   When it is considered desirable that some members not participate in discussing and deciding a *protest* or request for redress, and no qualified replacements are available, the jury remains properly constituted if at least three members remain. At least two members shall be International Judges.

N3.3   Members shall not be regarded as *interested parties* (see rule 63.4) by reason of their nationality.

N3.4   If a panel fails to agree on a decision it may adjourn and refer the matter to the full jury.

APPENDIX P – IMMEDIATE PENALTIES FOR BREAKING RULE 42

This appendix applies only if the sailing instructions so state.

P1 PROTESTS

A member of the protest committee or its designated observer who sees a boat breaking rule 42 may protest her by, as soon as reasonably possible, making a sound signal, pointing a yellow flag at her and hailing her sail number, even if she is no longer *racing*. A boat so protested is not subject to another *protest* under rule 42 for the same incident.

P2 PENALTIES

P2.1 First Protest

When a boat is first protested under rule P1 she may acknowledge her breach by taking a Two-Turns Penalty under rule 44.2. If she fails to do so she shall be disqualified without a hearing.

P2.2 Second Protest

When a boat is protested a second time during the series she may acknowledge her breach by immediately retiring from the race. If she fails to do so she shall be disqualified without a hearing and her score shall not be excluded.

P2.3 Third Protest

When a boat is protested a third time during the series she may acknowledge her breach by immediately retiring from the race and from all other races in the series. If she fails to do so she shall be disqualified without a hearing from all races in the series, with no score excluded, and the protest committee shall consider calling a hearing under rule 69.1(a).

P3 POSTPONEMENT, GENERAL RECALL OR ABANDONMENT

If a boat has been protested under rule P1 and the race committee signals a *postponement*, general recall or *abandonment*, the penalty from her first or second *protest* is cancelled, but the *protest* is counted to determine the number of times she has been protested during the series.

Received by race office: Number .... Date and time .... Signed ....

PROTEST FORM – also for requests for redress and reopening

Fill in and tick as appropriate

1. EVENT .... Organizing authority .... Date .... Race no ....

2. TYPE OF HEARING

Protest by boat against boat	❏	Request for redress by boat or race committee ❏
Protest by race committee against boat	❏	Consideration of redress by protest committee ❏
Protest by protest committee against boat	❏	Request by boat or race committee to reopen hearing ❏
		Consideration of reopening by protest committee ❏

3. BOAT PROTESTING, OR REQUESTING REDRESS OR REOPENING

Class .... Sail no .... Boat's name ....
Represented by .... Address ....Tel., e-mail .

4. BOAT(S) PROTESTED OR BEING CONSIDERED FOR REDRESS

Class .... Sail no .... Boat's name ....

5. INCIDENT

Time and place of incident ....
Rules alleged to have been broken .... Witnesses ....

6. INFORMING PROTESTEE How did you inform the protestee of your intention to protest?

By hailing	❏	When? .... Word(s) used........................
By displaying a red flag	❏	When? ....
By informing her in some other way	❏	....Give details

7. DESCRIPTION OF INCIDENT (use another sheet if necessary)

DIAGRAM: one square = hull length; show positiion of boats, wind and current directions, marks

....

....

....

....

....

....

....

....

....

....

....

THIS SIDE FOR PROTEST COMMITTEE USE Number .... Heard together with numbers ..

Fill in and tick as appropriate

Withdrawal requested ❑ ; Signature .... Withdrawal permitted ❑

Protest time limit ....

Protest, or request for redress or reopening, is within time limit ❑ Time limit extended ❑

Protestor, or party requesting redress or reopening, represented by ....

Other party, or boat being considered for redress, represented by ....

Names of witnesses ....

Interpreters ....

Remarks

Objection about interested party ❑ ....

Written protest or request identifies incident ❑ ....

'Protest' hailed at first reasonable opportunity ❑ ....

No hail needed; protestee informed at first reasonable opportunity ❑ ....

Red flag conspicuously displayed at first reasonable opportunity ❑ ....

Protest or request valid; hearing will continue ❑ Protest or request invalid; hearing is closed ❑

FACTS FOUND ....

....

....

....

....

....

....

Diagram of boat .... is endorsed by committee ❑   Committee's diagram is attached

❑

CONCLUSIONS AND RULES THAT APPLY

....

....

....

DECISION

Protest: dismissed ❑   Boat(s) .... is (are) disqualified

❑ ;

                                    penalized as follows ❑ : ....

Redress: not given ❑ ;   given as follows ❑ : ....

Request to reopen a hearing: denied ❑ ;   granted ❑

Protest committee chairman and other members ....

Chairman's signature .... Date and time ....

DEFINITIONS

A term used as stated below is shown in italic type or, in preambles, in bold italic type.

Abandon   A race that a race committee or protest committee *abandons* is void but may be resailed.

Clear Astern and Clear Ahead; Overlap   One boat is *clear astern* of another when her hull and equipment in normal position are behind a line abeam from the aftermost point of the other boat's hull and equipment in normal position. The other boat is *clear ahead*. They *overlap* when neither is *clear astern*. However, they also *overlap* when a boat between them *overlaps* both. These terms do not apply to boats on opposite tacks unless rule 18 applies.

Finish   A boat *finishes* when any part of her hull, or crew or equipment in normal position, crosses the finishing line in the direction of the course from the last *mark*, either for the first time or after taking a penalty under rule 31.2 or 44.2 or, under rule 28.1, after correcting an error made at the finishing line.

Interested Party   A person who may gain or lose as a result of a protest committee's decision, or who has a close personal interest in the decision.

Keep Clear   One boat *keeps clear* of another if the other can sail her course with no need to take avoiding action and, when the boats are *overlapped* on the same *tack*, if the *leeward* boat can change course in both directions without immediately making contact with the *windward* boat.

Leeward and Windward   A boat's *leeward* side is the side that is or, when she is head to wind, was away from the wind. However, when sailing by the lee or directly downwind, her *leeward* side is the side on which her mainsail lies. The other side is her *windward* side. When two boats on the same *tack overlap*, the one on the *leeward* side of the other is the *leeward* boat. The other is the *windward* boat.

Mark   An object the sailing instructions require a boat to leave on a specified side, and a race committee boat surrounded by navigable water from which the starting or finishing line extends. An anchor line and objects attached temporarily or accidentally to a *mark* are not part of it.

Obstruction   An object that a boat could not pass without changing course substantially, if she were sailing directly towards it and one of her hull lengths from it. An object that can be safely passed on only one side and an area so designated by the sailing instructions are also *obstructions*. However, a boat *racing* is not an *obstruction* to other boats unless they are required to *keep clear* of her, give her *room* or, if rule 21 applies, avoid her.

Overlap   See **Clear Astern** and **Clear Ahead; Overlap**.

Party   A party to a hearing: a protestor; a protestee; a boat requesting redress; a boat or a competitor that may be penalized under rule 69.1; a race committee or an organizing authority in a hearing under rule 62.1(a).

Postpone   A *postponed* race is delayed before its scheduled start but may be started or *abandoned* later.

Proper Course   A course a boat would sail to *finish* as soon as possible in the absence of the other boats referred to in the rule using the term. A boat has no *proper course* before her starting signal.

Protest   An allegation made under rule 61.2 by a boat, a race committee or a protest committee that a boat has broken a *rule*.

Racing   A boat is *racing* from her preparatory signal until she *finishes* and clears the finishing line and *marks* or retires, or until the race committee signals a general recall, *postponement* or *abandonment*.

Room   The space a boat needs in the existing conditions while manoeuvring promptly in a seamanlike way.

Rule (a) The rules in this book, including the Definitions, Race Signals, Introduction, preambles and the rules of relevant appendices, but not titles;

(b) ISAF Regulation 19, Eligibility Code; Regulation 20, Advertising Code; and Regulation 21, Anti-Doping Code;

(c) the prescriptions of the national authority, unless they are changed by the sailing instructions in compliance with the national authority's prescription, if any, to rule 87;

(d) the class rules (for a boat racing under a handicap or rating system, the rules of that system are 'class rules');

(e) the notice of race;

(f) the sailing instructions; and

(g) any other documents that govern the event.

Start   A boat *starts* when, having been entirely on the pre-start side of the starting line at or after her starting signal, and having complied with rule 30.1 if it applies, any part of her hull, crew or equipment crosses the starting line in the direction of the first *mark*.

Tack, Starboard or Port   A boat is on the *tack, starboard* or *port*, corresponding to her *windward* side.

Two-Length Zone   The area around a *mark* or *obstruction* within a distance of two hull lengths of the boat nearer to it.

Windward   See **Leeward** and **Windward.**

RACE SIGNALS

The meanings of visual and sound signals are stated below. When a visual signal is displayed over a class flag, the signal applies only to that class.

AP Races not started are *postponed*. The warning signal will be made 1 minute after removal unless at that time the race is postponed again or abandoned.

AP over a numeral pennant 1–6: *Postponement* of 1–6 hours from the scheduled starting time.

AP over H: Races not started are *postponed*. Further signals ashore.

AP over A: Races not started are *postponed*. No more racing today.

C The position of the next *mark* has been changed.

I Rule 30.1 is in effect.

L Ashore: A notice to competitors has been posted.
Afloat: Come within hail or follow this boat.

M The object displaying this signal replaces a missing *mark*.

N All races that have started are *abandoned*. Return to the starting area. The warning signal will be made 1 minute after removal unless at that time the race is abandoned again or postponed.

N over H: All races are *abandoned*. Further signals ashore.

N over A: All races are *abandoned*. No more racing today.

P Preparatory signal.

S The course has been shortened. Rule 32.2 is in effect.
At a rounding or finishing *mark: Finish* between the nearby *mark* and the staff displaying this flag.

X Individual recall.

Y Wear personal buoyancy.

Z Rule 30.2 is in effect.

First substitute: General recall. The warning signal will be made 1 minute after removal.

Black flag: Rule 30.3 is in effect.

Blue flag or shape: This Race Committee boat is in position at the finishing line.